Transform your church

Transform your church

50 **very** practical steps

Paul Beasley-Murray

INTER-VARSITY PRESS
38 De Montfort Street, Leicester LE1 7GP, England
Email: ivp@ivp-editorial.co.uk
Website: www.ivpbooks.com

First published 2005

British Library Cataloguing in Publication Data
A catalogue record for this book is available from the British Library.

ISBN-10: 1-84474-085-4
ISBN-13: 978-1-84474-085-7

Set in Dante 10.5/13pt
Typeset in Great Britain by CRB Associates, Reepham, Norfolk
Printed and bound in Great Britain by Ashford Colour Press Ltd, Gosport,
Hampshire.

*Inter-Varsity Press is the publishing division of the Universities and
Colleges Christian Fellowship (formerly the Inter-Varsity Fellowship),
a student movement linking Christian Unions in universities and
colleges throughout Great Britain, and a member movement of the
International Fellowship of Evangelical Students. For more information
about local and national activities write to UCCF, 38 De Montfort Street,
Leicester LE1 7GP, email us at email@uccf.org.uk, or visit the UCCF
website at www.uccf.org.uk.*

To Caroline,
with love

Contents

Introduction

The origins of this book go back to August 2003 when I suggested to Hazel Southam, the editor of the *Baptist Times*, the idea of writing a series of short articles relating to church life at the grass roots. In a letter to her I wrote:

> As a minister of a local church, I know how easy it is to become isolated – my experience very easily becomes confined to my church. In such a situation it makes such a difference to read how others 'do' church, not in order to adopt ideas wholesale, but to take and adapt that which would be appropriate. What is true of ministers, I think would also be true of other leaders in the church.

Hazel happily accepted my proposal, with the result that over the past year or so every week an article has appeared in which I reflected on an issue relating to life in the local church.

This series was named (by Hazel) *The Final Word* for the simple reason that they were the 'final word' at the bottom of the back page of the *Baptist Times*. Unfortunately, some have drawn the conclusion that I am claiming to have 'the final word' on all matters of church life. As one irate pastor wrote in to the paper, 'Paul, you are entitled to your opinion, but please, please, do not let us pretend that you have the final authoritative word ...'

In no way do I claim to have 'the final word' for the life of any church. Every church is different, and rightly so. Hopefully, however, my articles, couched often in deliberately provocative terms, will stimulate churches and their leaders to take a fresh look at themselves and their mission.

The editor's ruling was that my articles be around five hundred words each. As the series developed, it became clear that their brevity whetted the appetite of some for more. So what I have done is allow the original articles to appear as they were first written, and then I have supplemented each article with further material.[1]

I do not pretend that the articles cover every area of church life. They simply reflect my views on the topics upon which I was asked to write.

At the end of each chapter I have also provided five Scripture passages for reflection to make the book useful for discussion in small groups. It was suggested to me that many of the issues I have raised are rarely talked about in church life – and yet need to be.

Although the original series of articles was addressed to a Baptist audience, this book has the wider Christian church in view. For the vast majority of issues I have tackled are relevant to all churches, whatever their tradition. Certainly, the material supplementing the original articles is general in nature.

From the very first I had in mind the interests of ministers and other church leaders – although to my delight many ordinary church members have clearly enjoyed my contributions too. IVP have encouraged me to aim the book even more specifically at church leaders, with a view to making it more of a 'handbook' for leaders. Certainly, much of my supplementary material is focused on the needs of church leaders. The title *Transform Your Church! Fifty very practical steps*, together with the somewhat directive headings of the 50 chapters, all reflect this leadership emphasis. My one concern, however, in adopting this more directive approach is that it might appear that I am setting myself up as a leader with all the gifts of the archangel Gabriel himself. The fact is that, like any other minister in pastoral charge, I am still a learner. Furthermore, the church I am privileged to lead is still on a journey – as a church too we still have much to learn. My prayer, however, is that in spite of these limitations, the stimulus I seek to give might enable churches to have a greater impact on the communities they serve. If transformation is the result, then to God alone be the glory!

Part 1: Ministry

1. Maintain a devotional life

The editor asked me to write about what a minister's devotional life should be like, but there is no way in which I would wish to dictate the shape of another minister's devotional life. The precise nature of a minister's walk with God varies from minister to minister, and from one season to another in the life of a minister. So, instead of writing about others, let me write about my own devotional life. I confess that I do so with some reluctance, for I am still a learner on the Way – but then, aren't we all?

The traditional evangelical morning Quiet Time is at the heart of my devotional life. The first thing I do at the beginning of my working day is to read the Scriptures and to pray. Over the years my pattern has varied. Like many others, I have experimented using such tools as the North American *The Minister's Prayer Book*[1] and the Franciscan *Celebrating Common Prayer*,[2] but helpful as they are, I find the need to jump from one chapter of the book to another distracting. At other times I have read through particular books of the Bible with the aid of a commentary – some of the best such commentaries for devotional use are found in the IVP Bible Speaks Today series. The drawback here is that much of the time is taken up with the thoughts of the commentator rather than to the Word of

God itself. I know that some ministers follow the Robert Murray M'Cheyne Bible-reading plan, recently popularized in Don Carson's *For the Love of God*,[3] which takes the reader through the New Testament and Psalms twice and the Old Testament once – but that involves reading a lot of Scripture every day.

My own preferred option now is to use the Anglican *Common Worship* lectionary. Sometimes I read the set 'offices' of the day, with its two readings from the Old and New Testaments; but normally I stay with the three shorter passages set for 'Holy Communion' and which always include part of a psalm. I find that the lectionary gives me a balanced diet, yet it does not over-face me in terms of the amount. As I read, whenever a phrase or a verse jumps out at me, I mark my Bible – and then, for a shorter or longer period, I seek to chew over what God may be saying to me.

From Scripture I turn to prayer. Again, as with Bible-reading, so too with praying, I find the need for a system. I have devised a simple plan for the week, with eight main categories for each day: my family, my colleagues, my deacons (I split their names over the week), church activities, life beyond the local church (this includes such sub-categories as regional ministers and members of my local Baptist ministers' fellowship), 'Yesterday', 'Today' and 'Special Needs'.

To some this may seem over-structured, but for me the words of Henri Nouwen ring true: 'A spiritual life without discipline is impossible. Discipline is the other side of discipleship.'[4]

Encourage your people to have a Quiet Time

In response to a request from a member of my congregation, I spelled out in our church magazine eight simple steps as an aid for a Quiet Time:

1. Make time in your day when you can be quiet before God. For most people the early morning is best. True, we can speak to God as we walk down the street, as we drive along in the car, and even as we do the washing up. But those moments are bonuses and do not replace the need for a regular 'appointment' with God. That appointment doesn't have to be long – but it has to be there.

2. Find a space where you can spend time with God in a relaxed manner and without interruption. For young people their bedroom may be the only private place they have in their home. Others may

have a particular room or corner of a room or even a special chair where they like to be quiet. Some people make the place where they pray feel special by placing there a text or a small wooden cross or even a candle. Ideally, it should be a place where one can leave a Bible together with a notebook and a pen. If it is impossible to find any quiet at home, why not consider popping into a church on the way to work?

3. Then come to God, and begin your Quiet Time by asking that he will speak to you. With the psalmist say:

Open my eyes, so that I may behold
   wondrous things out of your law.
(Psalm 119:18)

4. Allow God to speak when you open your Bible and read a passage from it. Don't, however, open your Bible at whim and read 'any old' passage. Adopt a system for reading the Bible. Although one can develop one's own system, it is much easier to use one of the many systems on offer. The advantage of a Bible-reading system is that it offers a balanced diet – to begin with Genesis and read right through to Revelation is asking for spiritual indigestion. Many like to use Bible reading notes, which along with the reading for the day offer some words of explanation and suggestions for application. These notes are usually very good, but if you do use them, make sure you read the Scripture and not just the notes!

5. Listen for what God is saying to you through that Scripture by reading through the passage slowly – take time to reflect on a verse, a phrase or perhaps even just a word. A hasty reading of the Bible does little good. We need to discipline ourselves to 'meditate' on God's Word – to chew it over as a cow chews the cud. I always have with me a ruler and pencil, so that I can underline whatever jumps out from the text. Alternatively, write down in a book the thoughts that come to mind. This is also a good way of dealing with distracting thoughts – as well as helping to remember what God may be saying. Indeed, those so-called 'distracting' thoughts may actually be a way of God speaking to you.

6. Reading the Scripture naturally leads into prayer. In a sense the praying has already begun. For as we listen to God speaking through

his Word, we are in fact already praying, whether or not our eyes are closed. Prayer is more than our speaking to God – it is also God speaking to us. Now, we respond to what God has said to us. Normally, this response involves praise, thanksgiving or perhaps confession. (Note the old mnemonic: 'ACTS' – Adoration, Confession, Thanksgiving, Supplication.) Reading the Bible before praying tends to give specificity to one's adoration, confession and thanksgiving.

7. Now move into 'supplication', and pray for others – as also for yourself. Just as with Bible reading, so with praying, many Christians find it helpful to have a system, which may well involve making a prayer list.

8. Finally, before the day really gets going, take an opportunity to reflect on the priorities for the day. This is a time to make lists of things to do – or to review previous lists!

These eight steps make the daily Quiet Time seem a complicated operation, yet it is only as complicated as tying a shoelace (you try to describe all the steps involved in that daily habit). Once you have got into the rhythm, the discipline involved ceases to be a chore, and becomes simply a means of drawing upon God and his grace.

Scriptures to reflect on
- 'In all your ways acknowledge him, / and he will make straight your paths' (Proverbs 3:6).
- 'In the morning, while it was still very dark, he got up and went out to a deserted place, and there he prayed' (Mark 1:35).
- 'I am the vine, you are the branches. Those who abide in me and I in them bear much fruit, because apart from me you can do nothing' (John 15:5).
- 'Your word is truth' (John 17:17).
- 'Do not worry about anything, but in everything by prayer and supplication with thanksgiving let your requests be made known to God' (Philippians 4:6).

2. Aim for faithfulness, not results!

In the first seventy or so years of the twentieth century, Baptists, along with other denominations, lost two-thirds of their membership. Then, when church decline was the order of the day, it was sufficient for a Baptist minister to be 'faithful'. In those days ministers drew some comfort from the second half of Isaiah 6, where God tells the prophet that people will take no notice of what he has to say.

Today, however, the climate has changed. The massive decline we Baptists once experienced has stopped, thank God, and overall our churches are now just about holding our own. Indeed, some of our Baptist churches are experiencing dramatic growth. As a result, church growth has become the order of the day. People expect their ministers not just to be faithful, but to be 'fruitful'. Indeed, it has not been unknown for ministers to be asked to leave their church for failing to produce sufficient new members. Church growth – for the most part quite unfairly – has become the yardstick of a minister's worth. This makes it all the more tough for ministers when their churches fail to grow.

At this point let me go into personal testimony mode – indeed, the initial title given to me by the editor for this piece ('How do you handle lack of growth in your church?') calls for personal honesty. At one stage my ministry went through a lean period, and at the time I freely confess that I found the subsequent lack of growth difficult to handle. My first church had quadrupled in size during the thirteen years of my ministry there, so that when I came to my second church I had every expectation that growth would again characterize my ministry. But to my astonishment the reverse initially proved to be the case – a radical cull of the church roll together with deaths, resignations and people moving away resulted in substantial numerical decline. Thank God, over the last three years the tide has now well and truly turned: visitors abound and baptisms are up; the size of our Sunday morning congregation is now a problem; and, even as I write, some fourteen people are asking for membership. But, there was a stage when I almost despaired of the church. How did I then cope? By rediscovering Christ's call to go the way of the cross.

Gosh, that sounds incredibly pious – but nonetheless, that was the truth of the matter. As a result of going on retreat I was reminded again of the call of Jesus to 'follow me', and not to allow myself to be bothered by the 'successes' of others. This did not mean that I then took no notice of what 'successful' pastors like Bill Hybels of Willowcreek and Rick Warren of Saddleback had to say, but it does mean that I don't feel any pressure to model myself on them. Jesus, and Jesus alone, is our model – and, dare I say it without appearing too self-righteous, I have discovered again that his grace, is more than sufficient.[1]

Don't live on false expectations of ministry

There is nothing wrong with young ministers dreaming of doing great things for God, but dreams alone will not sustain ministry. For there are times when those dreams will be shattered.

One of the unrealistic pressures, often as much self-imposed as imposed by others, is the pressure to 'succeed' in ministry. Yet success in worldly in terms is not the ultimate yardstick of ministry. Ultimately, it is faithfulness to Jesus. We see this in the recommissioning of Peter. As Gordon Bridger commented:

> Love for Christ is the only motive that will keep the Christian
> disciple faithful to Christ, whatever the circumstances. It is not enough

to want to be successful, or want to do good in the world, or to leave the world a better place. We can easily be disillusioned if that is our motive for Christian service. Jesus wants to make sure we love him.[2]

Not only do many young ministers have a false expectation of their call; they often have a false expectation of the people they serve. The fact is that the sheep in their care will not always be loving and cuddlesome, but rather, like the sheep on the hills, they can be dirty and pest-ridden, silly and stupid. Sin is as much present in the church as without. Ministry is tough, precisely because, in spite of all the many wonderful sermons preached, people will continue to go their own selfish and loveless way! There are times when reason might well say: 'Throw the towel in. Go back to a steady job that does not demand every hour God gives, that does not leave you to the mercy of people's fanciful whims and unrealistic expectations.' But has ministry ever been a reasonable calling?

Another false expectation is to regard the pastoral ministry as a job. It is not a job – it is a calling. To confuse a calling with a job leads to confusion. In the words of Derek Tidball:

> Pastoral ministry ... is essentially about relationships, not about contracts ... The failure to understand this has been the reason, I believe, for the inability of a number of younger ministers to sustain ministry after a few years. Dissatisfaction with ministry often develops early. But this is not surprising if it is entered with wrong expectations. If either the fledgling pastor or the calling church pretends it can be approached like any other job, then it is not surprising if disappointment quickly follows. We can do no service to anyone by pretending the pastoral ministry can ever be like a nine-to-five job. By its nature it is different.[3]

> [That is, what is needed is] a rediscovery of a sense of pastoral vocation.[4]

Ministry is tough – but it is not helped by the presence of false expectations.

Scriptures to reflect on

- 'Peter ... said to Jesus, "Lord, what about him?" Jesus said ... "Follow me!"' (John 21:21–22).
- 'It is required of stewards that they be found trustworthy' (1 Corinthians 4:2).
- 'We have this treasure in clay jars, so that it may be made clear that this extraordinary power belongs to God and does not come from us. We are afflicted in every way, but not crushed ...' (2 Corinthians 4:7–8).
- 'I want to know Christ and the power of his resurrection and the sharing of his sufferings ...' (Philippians 3:10).
- 'Whenever you face trials of any kind, consider it nothing but joy, because you know that the testing of your faith produces endurance; and let endurance have its full effect, so that you may be mature and complete ...' (James 1:2–4).

3. Work – and play – hard!

Unlike most mortals, ministers have no set hours of work. Instead of a nine-to-five job, churches often seem to expect them to be at work 24 hours a day.

The story is told of how members of one church were given a questionnaire in which they were asked to state how many hours they felt their pastor should devote to the following tasks: administration, sermon preparation, evangelism visitation, youth work, counselling and personal prayer. The totals on the answers averaged 82 hours per week. Even though a week has only 168 hours, one member actually proposed 200 hours a week. Clearly, such expectations are totally unreasonable. So, what then is a reasonable workload? To what extent should churches be encouraging ministers to observe the European Working Time Directive, which limits the average weekly work time to 48 hours – although individuals can choose to work longer?

In most churches ministers still have only one day off a week – since almost everybody else has two days a week off, should not all churches now ensure that their ministers take off two days too? These are difficult questions to answer.

The difficulty lies in the fact that I do not consider myself an employee of the church: instead, I am an office-holder, set free by the church to devote myself to the ministry and mission of the church. For me ministry is not about 'rights', but about 'privilege'.

Last year I kept a careful time log for seven weeks: I discovered that in that period I averaged 57 hours a week. It was, of course, my choice – my privilege, if you like – to work that hard. I certainly do not feel that my church has any right to expect me to work that number of hours.

A different approach to determining a minister's workload is not to count hours at all, but rather to count time blocks. Each week has twenty-one time blocks: each week consists of seven days of three sessions a day. An employed person in a secular job normally works five days and two sessions per day – ten sessions a week. Therefore a minister should at the very least work ten sessions a week – and probably a good deal more. A minister friend of mine, however, argues that ministers should work fifteen sessions a week. His reasoning is as follows: if, in addition to the ten sessions per week taken up by his normal employment, a member attends church twice a Sunday, the total becomes twelve sessions; a deacon or other church officer might spend two evenings a week on church business; the minister should pave the way and do three – hence fifteen sessions. This leaves six sessions (two days) clear!

Gosh, I feel I have set the cat among the pigeons![1]

Ministers need breaks

Although there are some ministers who don't work hard enough, most work far too hard. Most ministers need to be encouraged to take a break.

The fact is that relaxation is part of being a man or woman of God. To be a person of compassion is not necessarily to be strung out by every human need that comes along. Sometimes 'No' needs to be said in order that caring can continue. The Greeks had a proverb: 'The bow that is always bent [always stretched taut] will soon cease to shoot straight.'

The example of Jesus is significant. On one occasion notable for its busyness Mark records that there were so many people coming and going that Jesus and his disciples 'had no leisure even to eat'. Jesus said to his disciples: 'Come away to a deserted place all by yourselves and rest a while' (Mark 6:31). Here Jesus exemplifies a doctrine of rest!

To paraphrase the words of the Preacher: 'There is a time for everything . . . A time to work, and a time not to work.'

Relaxation needs to be viewed as a discipline. It is part of God's order for humankind that one day in seven should be set aside for rest. God's order should be respected. Clearly, Sundays cannot be a day of rest for ministers – another day instead must be found. Traditionally, Monday has been the minister's day off. However, Monday is not necessarily the best day to take off: in my experience, at least, all kinds of pastoral matters come to my attention on a Sunday, so that on a Monday there is always so much to do. My own preference is to go for a Friday – not least because with a working wife Friday evenings are the end of her working week and so she can afford to be more relaxed. So, unless there is a funeral, Fridays tend to be sacrosanct.

Along with the weekly day off, holidays too are important. With the pressures of ministerial life, I'm a great believer in having a long summer holiday. I know that there are some ministers who take off a week here and a week there, but for my money a holiday needs to be at least three weeks long if it is to be a true break – for, many of us find it takes a week to forget the church. Traditionally, ministers have taken off the whole of August, and in my judgment rightly so. But time too needs to be taken off after Christmas and after Easter. Busy pastors (for their own sake, for the sake of their families, and ultimately for the sake of their churches) need to ensure that regular holidays are built into their diaries.

Scriptures to reflect on

- 'The sabbath was made for humankind' (Mark 2:27).
- 'Come away to a deserted place all by yourselves and rest a while' (Mark 6:31).
- 'Work hard and do not be lazy' (Romans 12:11, Good News Bible).
- 'For to me, living is Christ' (Philippians 1:21).
- 'For this I toil and struggle with all the energy that he powerfully inspires within me' (Colossians 1:29).

4. Welcome annual appraisals

It is my conviction that appraisals should be a way of life for pastors. As I write, I am looking forward to my tenth ministerial appraisal. In preparation for this I will have to submit a detailed review of the past year as also propose a number of key objectives for the following year. I will also review the opportunities for training and development, and share ideas for my future development.

My appraisers will be the church's Senior Deacon and the Pastoral Deacon – normally we have also invited a minister from outside the church to be involved in the process, but this year we have decided that a 'lighter' approach would be more appropriate. Needless to say, the content of the appraisal is strictly confidential – nothing is shared with anybody else without the express permission of all concerned. I have no doubt that this year's appraisal will again be a good experience.

Sadly, many ministers feel threatened by the prospect of appraisal. Believing themselves to be primarily accountable to God, they do not want to have to give account of their ministry to another. But if the word 'love' in 1 John 4:20 is changed to 'accountable', we find: 'We cannot be accountable to God whom we have not seen, if we are not willing to be accountable to our brother and sister whom we have seen'!

If only ministers were to appreciate that appraisal, properly handled, is a positive experience with their interests in mind. In many ways appraisal is more helpful to ministers than almost any other group of workers. For ministry is by and large a lonely profession. Unlike other professionals, ministers for the most part do not work together in teams – they are on their own. True, they are part of a local church, but most deacons have no real idea of what is involved in the day-to-day ministry of their pastors. What a difference it makes to be able to share in confidence some of the pressures we face. Annual appraisals can break down some of the isolationism and, in so doing, prove to be extremely supportive.

Annual appraisals are also intended to be a place for encouragement. They provide an opportunity for the appraiser(s) to affirm the pastor, to look back over the past and say 'Well done'; and then in the light of the past year set fresh goals for the coming year.

In addition, annual appraisals provide an opportunity for any difficulties to be picked up at an early stage and dealt with appropriately. In this sense appraisals may be likened to a form of preventative medicine. Within the context of reviewing a person's ministry, a skilled appraiser can discern areas that, without attention, might lead to subsequent disaster. Appraisals provide an opportunity for early diagnosis of problems. They also provide a safe place for the kind of straight talking that is not otherwise normally possible. It is important, however, to emphasize that in the first place appraisals, rightly conducted, are positive, upbuilding experiences.[1]

Benefiting from appraisal

Appraisals are immensely beneficial and are to be welcomed, and not feared. In the words of a report on appraisal by the Division of Ordained Ministry of the United Methodist Church of America:

> Evaluation is natural to the human experience. Evaluation is one of God's ways of bringing the history of the past into dialogue with the hope for the future. Without confession of sin there is no reconciliation; without the counting of blessings there is no thanksgiving; without the acknowledgement of accomplishments there is no celebration; without awareness of potential there is no hope; without hope there is no desire for growth; without desire for growth the past will dwarf the future.

We are called into new growth and new ministries by taking a realistic and hopeful look at what we have been and what we can still become. Surrounded by God's grace and the crowd of witnesses in the faith, we can look at our past unafraid and from its insights eagerly face the future with new possibilities.[2]

There are, however, difficulties with the appraisal of ministers. One difficulty is found in the fact that very rarely is there a written job description. It is assumed everyone knows what ministers do and what is required of them. The reality is that there are a variety of approaches to ministry. There are a variety of ways in which ministers may organize their time and determine their priorities.

Another difficulty in ministerial appraisal is that ministers for the most part are their own bosses. Technically employed by the church, in reality they act as leaders of the church. To whom are they accountable when it comes to appraisal?

A third difficulty is that the work of the 'performance' of the minister is intimately bound up with the 'performance' of the church. It is difficult to appraise the one without the other.

None of these difficulties is insuperable. For example, there is no reason why ministers should not be encouraged to produce their own job descriptions, which might form the basis for review. The second difficulty is a little more problematic. In one sense for the local church to evaluate its own minister is somewhat like patients evaluating their doctor. For this reason in some of the more hierarchical denominations 'line' appraisal is the norm, in which the appraisal is conducted by the archdeacon or equivalent functionary. The drawback, however, is that in so far as this involves an 'outsider' the appraisal is inevitably based on second-hand knowledge. An alternative is to engage in peer review with another minister or groups of ministers. To my mind the least satisfactory form of appraisal is self-assessment, for time and again we fail to see ourselves as we truly are. My own preference is for the appraisal to be conducted by the local church with a ministerial facilitator drawn from outside the fellowship. As for the third difficulty, a review of the church's ministry as a whole could be conducted at the same time as a review of the ministry of its pastor. However, this would be very time-demanding, and there would be the danger that for a significant period of the year the church could be distracted from its task of ministry as a result of this internal-auditing process. Perhaps one could envisage such a general evaluation taking place once every five years?

Over the years the shape of my appraisal document has varied. However, the following issues would normally be addressed:

1. *Statement of job purpose.* Highlight up to six of the most important areas.
2. *Review of last year's objectives.* What were the three main achievements last year? What areas could have been more effective?
3. *Review of development.* What learning has taken place and how is it being applied? What can be done to improve performance?
4. *Planning the coming year's objectives.* What are the priority areas of work during the next twelve months? These need to link with the church's objectives. They need also to be precise, measurable, achievable and have a timescale.
5. *Development plan.* What development opportunities are required to support the achievement of the minister's objectives within the current role, as also of the minister's aspirations for further long-term development?
6. *Other comments.* Are there other comments that you wish to express privately?

Scriptures to reflect on
- 'The wise listen to advice' (Proverbs 12:15).
- 'Iron sharpens iron' (Proverbs 27:17).
- 'All must test their own work' (Galatians 6:4).
- 'I press on towards the goal for the prize of the heavenly call of God in Christ Jesus' (Philippians 3:14).
- 'Let us consider how to provoke one another to love and good deeds, . . . encouraging one another' (Hebrews 10:24–25).

5. Build in regular retreats

Retreats are not a luxury, but a necessity for a minister's integrity. Just like cars need a general service every year, so too do ministers. Otherwise we risk under-performing, if not breaking down.

My last but one retreat was a personally guided semi-'Ignatian' retreat involving total withdrawal from the world – no phone calls, no listening to the radio, no watching TV, no reading the paper, no conversation with anybody apart from with a priest who specialized in spiritual direction. Every evening I met with him for an hour or so. At the end of our first meeting I was given three Scripture passages to form the basis of reflection the following day. All the next day I worked at those passages, meditating, praying, journalling, before meeting up with my spiritual director, who in the light of our conversation gave me a further three Scripture passages. It was a painful experience as day after day I found myself baring my soul to God. And so it went on, a whole week of doing business with God. By the end of the process I felt exhausted – and yet exhilarated.

This year I spent two weeks enjoying a body, mind and spirit focus with the Devon-based Society of Mary and Martha, who specialize in supporting ministers under stress. The fact is that far too many ministers suffer from the Martha syndrome and become distracted with much serving. Instead, like Mary, we need to sit down at the Lord's feet and listen to him. In their relaxed setting I was able to do that. I had time to read, to pray and to reflect; to do different walks every day; to snooze, to listen to the radio, even watch the TV; to enjoy a couple of massages; generally to unwind. It was a silent retreat, in the sense that although others were around, we were not encouraged to do more than say 'Hello' to one another. On my first full day I met with the two 'facilitators' – one theologically trained, the other medically trained. Thereafter I met with one or the other, six times in total.

The aim of the experience is summed up in the words of welcome given to each minister: 'Here may you lay aside burdens borne for self and others. May this place be for you a vessel of love, where from you may draw rest, silence, healing and vision. And may the Creator's love warmly glow from all that you see.' This was my experience. As a result, I have returned with a new spiritual dynamic, ready to face all the challenges of the coming year.

So, if you are a minister and have yet to experience a retreat, let me encourage you to discover the difference that time out with God can make; if you are not a minister, let me urge you to encourage your minister to go on retreat – it's a good investment for the church![1]

Look to Jesus

How do ministers maintain their sense of pastoral vocation? Surely by focusing on Jesus, the 'great shepherd of the sheep' (Hebrews 13:20). When I was a teenager we used to sing the chorus 'When the road is rough and steep, fix your eyes upon Jesus'. Not all chorus theology is sound, but that one certainly is! Jesus is our model for ministry. In tough times we need to look to him, and not to the models of ministry provided by Spring Harvest, Keswick or wherever.

We need to look to Jesus, for he is the one who will sustain us in ministry. In the words of the writer to the Hebrews:

> Keep your eyes on Jesus, who both began and finished this race we're in. Study how he did it. Because he never lost sight of where he was headed – that exhilarating finish in and with God – he could put up with anything along the way: cross, shame, whatever. And now he's there, in the place of honor, right alongside God. When you find

yourselves flagging in your faith, go over that story again, item by item, that long litany of hostility he plowed through. That will shoot adrenaline into your souls!
(Hebrews 12:2–4, *The Message*)

The very use of the name 'Jesus' here (as distinct from a title such as 'Christ' or 'Lord') should probably encourage us in the first place to look at the life of Jesus. 'The use of the simple personal name "Jesus" shows that the accent is upon his humanity, and especially his endurance of pain, humiliation and the disgrace of the cross.'[2] Jesus in the way in which he lived life set us a pattern for our living and for our ministry. He knew what it was like to be misunderstood, to experience opposition, to be rejected. There is nothing we have to endure that Jesus has not already endured.

As shepherds, ministers are but 'under-shepherds' of the 'great shepherd' (Hebrews 13:20). It is the one who said 'I am the good shepherd. The good shepherd lays down his life for the sheep' who is our ultimate model. In other words, pastoral ministry by definition is a costly calling. For unlike the hired hand who, when he sees the wolf coming, 'leaves the sheep and runs away – and the wolf snatches them and scatters them' (John 10:12), the good shepherd stays by his post, whatever the cost. The good shepherd is not motivated by self-interest, whether it be a wage-packet or self-preservation, but rather by concern for the sheep.

Although times have changed, the costliness of the call has not. It remains at the heart of pastoral ministry. The sacrifices of time and energy, of reputation and reward, are par for the course. In the words of Derek Tidball:

> Some seek a ministry without cost. But it is a sheer illusion to imagine that anyone could ever pastor in the image of the good shepherd and avoid any cost. Cost is inherent in the role. The costs of working long and unsociable hours, of being vulnerable, of being weak, of facing criticism, of being lonely, of being drained by people. Ministry takes it out of you ... Paying the cost is a sign of being an authentic shepherd.[3]

There have been times when I have wished Jesus were not my model for ministry; when I did not want to take up my cross and follow the crucified. It is all too painful. I want success, I want glory. But in the words of the old Negro spiritual: 'You cannot wear the crown if you do not bear the cross.' Jesus calls us to follow him. Thank God, we do not have to follow afar (for, to change the metaphor, he invites us to take his yoke upon us) to allow him to come alongside and experience his strength in dealing with the burdens of ministry.

William Temple, at his enthronement as Bishop of Manchester, said:

> I come as a learner, with no policy to advocate, no plan already formed to follow. But I come with one burning desire: it is that in all our activities, sacred and secular and ecclesiastical and social, we should help each other fix our eyes on Jesus, making him our only guide.[4]

Here are words for ministers to apply to themselves – and in so doing seek the prayers of their people.

Scriptures to reflect on
- 'Come to me, all you that are weary and are carrying heavy burdens, and I will give you rest. Take my yoke upon you, and learn from me . . .' (Matthew 11:28–29).
- 'If any want to become my followers, let them deny themselves and take up their cross and follow me' (Mark 8:34).
- 'Jesus, full of the Holy Spirit, returned from the Jordan and was led by the Spirit in the wilderness . . . At daybreak he departed and went into a deserted place' (Luke 4:1, 42).
- 'My grace is sufficient for you, for power is made perfect in weakness' (2 Corinthians 12:9).
- 'Let us run with perseverance . . . looking to Jesus' (Hebrews 12:1–2).

6. Stay for the long term – and keep fresh

Some years ago Alan Wilkinson and I discovered on the basis of a survey of some 350 English Baptist churches that 'it is not until a minister has served for five to ten years in his church that a bias towards growth becomes evident. In other words, it takes time for fruit to emerge from someone's leadership'.[1]

More recently Lynn Anderson, an American pastor, said of pastoral ministry:

> The first two years you can do nothing wrong. The second two years you can do nothing right. The fifth and sixth years of a ministry, either you leave or the people who think you can do nothing right, leave. Or you change, or they change, or you both change. Productive ministry emerges somewhere in the seventh year or beyond.[2]

If this is so, then most English Baptist ministers don't stay long enough in one church, for the average-length pastorate, according to the Baptist Union Directory, would appear to be around six years.

Of course, there are dangers in long pastorates – not least when the long-term pastorate has resulted by 'default'; for example, when a minister would like to move on to another church, but fails to get a call. Long-term ministry is not necessarily always fruitful ministry. There is no point, for instance, for a minister to remain in a church where the members as a whole refuse to follow the leadership offered; nor is there any point in remaining in a church where it quickly becomes apparent that one is a square peg in a round hole. As I reflect on my own experience of ministry, first of thirteen years in one church, and currently eleven years in another, I have found long-term ministry extremely rewarding and fulfilling. It's a wonderful privilege, for instance, to be involved with families over a period of time and to see those children brought for a service of dedication later confess their own faith in baptism; and then at a later stage to be involved in their marriage and even in the dedication of their children. There can be great gains in family stability: my own children benefited no end from spending their formative years in one happy church. And of course, there are also great gains in the development of deep and meaningful friendships; constantly shifting from one place to another can lead to ministers and their spouses experiencing fairly shallow relationships.

However, if long-term ministries are to become the norm, then the following two things are necessary. First of all, ministers need to free themselves from viewing ministry as a 'career', which involves constantly seeking to move to ever bigger and better churches. As Eugene Peterson rightly said: 'the congregation is not a job site to be abandoned when a better offer comes along'. Secondly, ministers need to commit themselves to growth and development in their own personal and professional lives – otherwise, they will become stale, and bore their churches rigid.[3]

The advantages of a long-term pastorate

According to some North American research, there are six positive advantages of a long-term pastorate:

- It makes possible greater in-depth knowledge of and relationships between the pastor and individual church members as well as between clergy and the congregation as a whole.
- It makes possible cumulative developing knowledge and experience of each other for both clergy and congregation, as they observe and participate in each other's growth over time.

- With greater continuity and stability of leadership and programme, it makes possible events not possible during a short tenure.
- It opens up possibilities of greater personal and spiritual growth for both clergy and congregation.
- It makes possible deeper knowledge of and participation by the clergy in the community (local, professional, ecumenical, larger denominational).
- It allows additional personal benefits for both the clergy and his/her family.[4]

But such advantages are not inevitable. The researchers conclude:

In many ways, maintaining a healthy long pastorate is more difficult than changing pastorates every five to eight years. Clergy can dazzle and even fool a congregation over shorter periods of ministry. Many simply repeat their five-year bag of tricks everywhere they go. In a long pastorate people get to know their clergy very well, both their assets and their liabilities. These clergy either need to be genuine, authentic persons who live by what they preach and advocate or, to the detriment of their ministry, they are soon found out. It is definitely easier to be the spiritual mentor of people over the short haul than over the long haul. In a long pastorate, clergy soon exhaust whatever wisdom or knowledge they brought to the scene and must continue to scramble to grow personally or end up repeating themselves and boring others. But those who do grow, who do monitor the other disadvantages of a long pastorate, will be likely to have a ministry that is very rewarding and fulfilling.[5]

If long-term pastorates rather than short-term pastorates are to become the norm, then there has to be a change of mindset on the part of pastors. They have to free themselves from viewing ministry as a 'career', which involves constantly seeking to move to a bigger and better church. Eugene Peterson tells of how when at the age of 30 he came to Christ Our King Presbyterian Church, Bel Air, Maryland, he determined to stay there for his entire ministry. Influenced by the Benedictine rule of 'stability' he saw the church as a place for developing 'vocational holiness'. As he came to the end of his twenty-four-year pastorate he wrote:

> I found a way to detach myself from the careerism mindset that has been so ruinous to pastoral vocations and began to understand my congregation as a location for a spiritually maturing life and ministry. I don't insist on the metaphor for others. I might be the only one for whom it works. I do insist, though, that the congregation is not a job site to be abandoned when a better offer comes along.[6]

Yet more than a mindset is called for. Longer pastorates will only be successful to the degree that ministers themselves are growing and developing. For this to happen pastors need others to help them grow and develop. Hopefully, the stimulus will in part come from within the local church – I have been fortunate to have had leaders who have contributed to my own growth and development. Certainly, there is something lacking if pastor and people cannot 'journey' together. However, outside resources are also vital. There is a limit to the extent to which ministers can make themselves vulnerable to their people. There are times when we need specialized help in our walk with God. Here 'soul friends' and 'spiritual directors' have a vital role to play. They also need help to grow and develop in their understanding and practice of ministry. For the church's sake (let alone for their own sake) pastors cannot afford to stand still. If churches are to be on the move, they too must be on the move. This is the secret of the effective long-term pastorate.

Scriptures to reflect on
- 'No one who puts a hand to the plough and looks back is fit for the kingdom of God' (Luke 9:62).
- Paul 'argued daily in the lecture hall of Tyrannus. This continued for two years, so that all the residents of Asia . . . heard the word of the Lord' (Acts 19:9–10).
- 'All of us . . . seeing the glory of the Lord as though reflected in a mirror, are being transformed into the same image from one degree of glory to another; for this comes from the Lord, the Spirit' (2 Corinthians 3:18).

- 'Rekindle the gift of God that is within you through the laying on of my hands' (2 Timothy 1:6).
- 'I have fought the good fight, I have finished the race, I have kept the faith' (2 Timothy 4:7).

7. Move only when God calls

In some denominations ministers have no choice – they are simply moved on at the allotted time. But we Baptists leave it to the individual minister to decide – unless, of course, things go terribly wrong and the minister is asked to leave. But how do ministers decide when is the time to move on?

Publicly ministers will speak of the way in which they have been *called* to move on to their next church, but if they were honest, many would acknowledge that often a host of very human factors underlie that call. For most ministers the call to move on does not come out of the blue; long before the calling church had been aware of them, they had asked the regional minister for their name to be put on the list of ministers wanting a move. So what motivates a minister to believe it right to move on?

Undoubtedly, some move on simply because they want a change – they have become bored with where they are. Is that a valid reason for moving on? Maybe. And yet does such boredom perhaps speak of a failure of self-development and growth?

Others move on because they feel that the church needs a different kind of leadership – they have taken the church so far, but they have not the gifts to move the church to the next stage. And that can well be a right and brave decision.

Yet others move on because they feel they are ready for a 'bigger challenge' – and by a 'bigger challenge' they mean a bigger church. But are there not times when the 'bigger challenge' would be to stay and help the church overcome whatever is holding it back?

Often ministers move on because things have become difficult in the church. But is it a sufficient reason to move on simply because the church seems resistant to one's ministry? Maybe there are times when ministers need to heed the words of Jesus to 'wipe the dust off their feet' and move on to those who will respect them. Yet let's not put all the blame on the church: it could be that the minister concerned has failed to manage the process of change. I am convinced that more ministers need to stay and endure the 'heat of the kitchen', for tough times do not last forever.

Some believe that the best time to leave is when things are going well: as one experienced minister said to me, the right time to move is when you are 'winning'.

There are times, however, when a call does come out of the blue. Some ministers are headhunted even though their name is not on the list. Others come to the attention of a church almost accidentally – holiday 'preaches' are particularly dangerous if the church visited is vacant!

Then, of course, there are other factors involved: on a very human level there are the educational and emotional needs of one's children; the needs of parents or of spouse; maybe too issues of health and energy. And along with all these human factors God speaks through prayer and through reflection on his Word, through advice of friends or through the pages of a challenging book. Discerning the call of God is indeed a complex business.[1]

Look for opportunity – and opposition too

When it came to considering the call to my present church, a verse of Scripture kept coming to my mind: 'a wide door for effective work has opened to me' (1 Corinthians 16:9), or as the Good News Bible puts it: 'There is a real opportunity here for great and worth-while work'. Initially, I didn't feel particularly 'called' to move to Chelmsford. I met with the deacons with reluctance, making clear that my heart really lay elsewhere; and when they invited me to come and 'preach with a view' (to the pastorate), I refused and said I would only come to preach, with no strings attached. But the more they persisted, the more God used this Scripture verse to convince me that Chelmsford was the place of his choosing.

At the time I disregarded the way in which Paul qualified his statement: 'even although there are many opponents' (Good News Bible). Indeed, in my eventual letter of acceptance of the call, I wrote: 'The Scripture that has come to my mind at this juncture is 1 Corinthians 16:9: "a wide door for effective work has opened to me" (fortunately, Paul's next few words are not applicable!).' But, as I discovered to my cost, I was wrong. The fact is that wherever there is opportunity for the gospel, there is always opposition. The Devil would not have it otherwise.

This was true of Paul's experience in Ephesus. Along with great opportunity for the gospel, Paul also experienced great opposition. So much so that he spoke of fighting with 'wild beasts' at Ephesus (1 Corinthians 15:32). This is not a reference to his being thrown to the lions. Rather, he was using a powerful metaphor to describe the kind of vicious opposition he faced.

Although Paul encountered difficulties with the silversmiths, the opposition Paul experienced sprang from the synagogue (see Acts 20:18–19): the religious establishment. Paul's experience was not unique. Time and again ministers find that opportunities for the gospel are thwarted by opposition from within the church. I'm reminded of the story of a young minister in his first church who went to visit the church's senior deacon: 'You must have seen a great many ministers.' 'Yes, and I've been against them all.'

The fact is that every church develops its own traditions. There is, of course, a place for tradition, but not if tradition stifles the Word of God. Traditional worship patterns can, for example, result in 'user-hostile' services. Traditional organization structures, which were good in their time, can obstruct the church from going out in mission.

One might expect that, of all people, Christians would be in favour of change; after all, 'repentance' is all about change. Alas, as David Cormack says, sometimes Christians can be the most resistant to change.

Since most Christian organizations continue to exist because of the favourable perception of their supporters rather than their necessary performance in the market-place of life, it is all too easy for them to succumb to the idea that their lack of progress is God's will for them. One of the roles of the change agent [i.e. the minister] is to help people see that God desires them to be growing not only in their individual lives, but in the life of their organization.[2]

So when it comes to considering a call elsewhere, by all means look for the opportunities. But at the same time be realistic: there will be opposition.

A few months ago I did a simple 'SWOT' analysis with my church:

Strengths – God is with us
Weaknesses – Our church is made up of fallible people like you and me
Opportunities – Galore
Threats – Many, but none insuperable

What was true of our church, is surely true of every church!

Scriptures to reflect on
- 'I will instruct you and teach you the way you should go ... / Do not be like a horse or a mule, without understanding, / whose temper must be cured with bit and bridle ...' (Psalm 32:8–9).
- 'They attempted to go into Bithynia, but the Spirit of Jesus did not allow them' (Acts 16:7).
- 'During the night Paul had a vision: there stood a man of Macedonia pleading with him and saying, "Come over to Macedonia and help us." When he had seen the vision, we immediately tried to cross over to Macedonia, being convinced that God had called us ...' (Acts 16:9–10).
- 'Now, as a captive to the Spirit, I am on my way to Jerusalem' (Acts 20:22).
- 'I will stay in Ephesus until Pentecost, for a wide door for effective work has opened to me, and there are many adversaries' (1 Corinthians 16:8–9).

Part 2: Church membership

8. Be committed to one another

In the 2001 Census, 72% of respondents described themselves as Christians, yet only some 7.5% of the population go to church every Sunday. Although I recognize that most of the 72% are what we might term 'nominal' Christians, I find it an encouraging statistic. It means, for instance, there is still a substantial church fringe, which might be open to attending Alpha courses and the like.

But what about the 7.5% of churchgoers? Are they the committed Christians as opposed to those who are Christians only in name? From a traditional Baptist perspective, the answer is 'No'. For we have always maintained that there's far more to Christian commitment than simply going to church – it involves commitment to Christ, which in turn involves commitment to his people. And just as our commitment to Christ should be wholehearted, so too should our commitment to his people be wholehearted.

That wholehearted understanding of commitment to Christ and his people is expressed by Baptists in church membership. When people become members of a Baptist church, they don't simply 'join' a church; they actually enter into a covenant with the people of God.

As I say every time I welcome people into membership: 'In a Baptist church, membership involves entering into a dynamic covenant relationship with one another – a relationship in which we commit ourselves not only to work together to extend Christ's kingdom, but also to love one another and stand by one another, whatever the cost.'

A church covenant is a bit like the covenant we make in marriage. In the wedding service we commit ourselves to one another: 'all that I am I give to you and all that I have I share with you'. The same too is true of church membership. In the words of Richard Sider, a covenant relationship involves 'an unconditional availability to and unlimited liability for the other brother or sister emotionally, financially and spiritually'. Furthermore, just as in the wedding service we take one another 'for better, for worse' – so too in the church. I never understand people who bale out when the going gets tough – commitment is the name of the game!

Rightly understood, when we vote upon applications for member-ship, we are not declaring that the applicants have come up to our 'standard' and are therefore 'worthy' to become members of our church. None of us is worthy, and the moment we believe otherwise, that moment we are not fit to belong to the church of God. No, in voting we are committing ourselves to stand by our new friends, come hell or high water.

Or to put it another way, a committed Christian is a person who takes seriously the 'new commandment' of Christ 'to love one another' just as he has loved us. Simply going to church is not a sign of commitment.[1]

Kissing frogs is the task of the church!

I collect frogs. Not real frogs (they unnerve me), but pretend frogs. I have frogs of stone, plastic, metal and material. To entertain little children entering my church office I have a *Little Frog Book* which features a large rubber frog that squeaks every time it is pushed. In my office I have a frog doorstop, a frog bookmark and frog pictures. You name it, I've got it. People in the 'know' help me with my frog collection. Sometimes they give me little frogs. At other times they send me froggy cards.

It probably all sounds very strange. There is, however, a very simple explanation. These frogs remind me of my calling – as indeed the calling of the church. Our task is to kiss frogs.

Has the penny dropped? If not, let me explain what I have in mind by developing my froggy theme, courtesy of a parable I came across in a book by the Australian John Mallison:

Have you ever felt like a frog? You know the type of thing I mean – stone cold, clammy, ugly, drooping, green, lifeless – all by yourself in the middle of a pond! I have! And I've met plenty of others. We have one in our house nearly every morning. The only thing missing is the pond!

The frog blues (or should I say greens) come when

- you want to be bright, especially first thing in the morning, and you can't
- you want to share, but are selfish
- you want to feel thankful, but feel resentment
- you want to be honest with others, but keep wearing a mask
- you want to be somebody, but feel a nobody
- you want to care, but the required effort makes you indifferent
- you want to make friends, but will they respond?

If we are honest we have probably all sat on that lily pad in the middle of the pond. Often we have sat there for ages, too frightened or disgusted to jump off and swim. Maybe you're still on that lily pond, floating around and round – all froggy like, fed up and lonely.

Others we meet . . . come across as frogs. They are so hard to love. Their personality doesn't attract others to them. They are either slow, shy, withdrawn and negative, or they are dominant, autocratic, forcing their opinions on others. Cold unattractive frogs. You feel repulsed by them and want to ignore or throw a rock at them.

A parable might help: Once upon a time there was a frog. He was really a handsome prince under the nasty spell of a wicked witch. Only the kiss of a beautiful maiden could save him. So there he sat – unkissed prince of his lily pond kingdom. But you've guessed it! One day a beautiful maiden saw him, was overcome with pity, grabbed him and kissed him. Bingo! In a moment of time he stood transformed before her, a handsome prince. And you can guess the finish!

SO WHAT is the task of the church? To KISS FROGS of course![2]

Churches are full of frogs. If I am honest I have met people in churches whom I would never choose to be friends. Some have come over as the weirdest of oddballs, while others can appear to be downright unlovely. And yet once I begin to put my mind to loving these characters, I discover that they are no longer as unlovable as they first appeared.

So when I've had a bad afternoon visiting or have sat through a difficult meeting, I retire to my office and see my frogs – and I remember that the task of the church is to kiss frogs. Frog-kissing isn't easy, but it can sometimes prove very rewarding.

Incidentally, a biblical justification for frog-kissing is found in the words of Jesus: 'I give you a new commandment, that you love one another. Just as I have loved you, you also should love one another. By this everyone will know that you are my disciples, if you have love for one another' (John 13:34–35).

Scriptures to reflect on
- 'Greet one another with a holy kiss' (Romans 16:16).
- 'Have the same care for one another' (1 Corinthians 12:25).
- 'Encourage one another and build one another up' (1 Thessalonians 5:11).
- 'Bear one another's burdens' (Galatians 6:2).
- 'Confess your sins to one another, and pray for one another, so that you may be healed' (James 5:16).

9. Develop deeper relationships

Too many churches are pervaded by a sense of unreality. My mind goes to the announcement often made in an English church 'After the service we will have a time of fellowship over a cup of tea and biscuits.' I feel like shouting out: 'Rubbish! That's not true.' For I have never experienced true fellowship over a church cup of tea and biscuits. I may have experienced a certain superficial friendliness – but real fellowship, never.

We Baptists are good at being friendly people – at offering cups of tea and maybe a chocolate biscuit too. Most of our churches, thank God, are not like that apocryphal church that was 'Gothic in architecture, arctic in temperature, and where the deacons walked up and down the aisles like polar bears!' No, our churches are generally characterized by a certain degree of warmth, which in itself can be very winsome. But fellowship is more than warmth, fellowship is more than being friendly. Fellowship is something that goes much deeper. Fellowship is about operating at levels two and one, rather than levels five, four and three.

Let me explain. Some years ago the American Jesuit John Powell in his book *Why Am I Afraid to Tell You Who I Am?* helpfully described five levels of conversation.

Level 5: Clichés – 'Terrible weather we're having these days!'
Level 4: Facts about others – 'Did you hear about Mrs So-and-So?'
Level 3: My ideas and judgments – 'Workers these days are only out for what they can get!'
Level 2: My feelings – 'I'm so relieved! I never realized that you felt that way about it.'
Level 1: Peak communication (absolute openness/honesty) – 'Our relationship hasn't been easy, but I want to tell you that I really value you as my friend.' [1]

Most people can operate at levels 5, 4 and 3 without too much difficulty. For example, level 5 is the kind of conversation we have with a stranger at a bus stop – or in a church pew. Level 4 is the kind of conversation we can have with an acquaintance ('gossip'), whether within or without the church. While level 3 is the kind of conversation that often goes on at the church meeting (except it's normally not about workers, but about young people: 'Young people these days are not what they were!' or 'Young people never leave the kitchen tidy'). But how often do ordinary members in the church really get down to levels 1 and 2, the levels of feeling and of peak communication? Rarely. Yet these levels are what real fellowship is all about.

Sadly, unless a church is prepared to structure its life around small groups, true fellowship will never really be possible. Honest conversations, meaningful relationships, will be the exception rather than the rule. It is only within the privacy of a small group, where people have begun to trust one another, that we can make ourselves vulnerable and so become real with one another. Small groups should not be optional extras in any church – they are an essential to being church. [2]

Encourage one another through small groups

William James said that 'the deepest principle in human nature is the craving to be appreciated'. We all need appreciation – we all need encouragement. As the Americans put it: 'We all need to be stroked.' The fact is that few of us remain on a perpetual even keel: all of us have our ups and downs; all of us need a brother or sister to speak a word of encouragement into our lives.

A legend is told of how God decided to reduce the weapons in the Devil's armoury. Satan could choose only one 'fiery dart'. He chose the power of discouragement. 'If only I can persuade Christians to be thoroughly discouraged, they will make no further effort and I will be enthroned in their lives.' The exercise of encouragement within the small group ensures that the Devil has no place.

Paul wrote to the Thessalonians: 'Encourage one another and build up each other' (1 Thessalonians 5:11). The context here was of death and bereavement. There were people in the church at Thessalonica who were finding the deaths of some of their friends hard to handle. Bereavement can be a shattering experience. Grieving isn't done within a matter of days – it goes on for months. Paul in such a context called upon the Thessalonians to encourage one another. Such encouragement today best takes place in the small group.

My mind goes back to the time I attended an American small group: it was the business meeting of my mother's Sunday School class. At that time my parents lived in Louisville, Kentucky, and were members of one of those superchurches with over 2,000, if not 3,000, members. That church was broken down into small groups, which in a Southern Baptist setting were known as 'All Age Sunday School classes'. My mother belonged to a class of women all of a similar age – at that time she was in her late fifties, and all the other women were of a similar age or a little older. When they met for their midweek business meeting the subject on the agenda was 'How do we care for one another, when a loved one dies?' Here they had in mind the death of a husband or the death of a parent. They were all of an age when such deaths were likely. I was amazed how for an hour or so – in a 'business meeting' – these women discussed how they could offer practical help encouragement to one another in time of bereavement. Here was love in action. This is what true fellowship is all about.

We can apply this injunction of Paul to encourage one another in a more general way. For death is not the only form of loss. Some parents experience a sense of loss when their children start school, and others experience a sense of loss when their children leave home. Redundancy is another form of loss, involving not only loss of a job, but also loss of status. In a similar way retirement can also be a form of loss. In all these situations (and many more) encouragement is needed. And the best place is the small group.

Scriptures to reflect on

- 'It is not good that the man should be alone' (Genesis 2:18).
- 'Day by day, as they spent much time together in the temple, they broke bread at home ...' (Acts 2:46).
- 'Rejoice with those who rejoice, weep with those who weep' (Romans 12:15).
- 'Encourage one another' (1 Thessalonians 4:18).
- 'Like good stewards of the manifold grace of God, serve one another ...' (1 Peter 4:10).

10. Preserve unity

For Baptists the church meeting is the occasion when we seek to discover God's pattern for our life together. In this seeking of the mind of Christ a bare majority is never sufficient. We look for consensus. However, consensus does not necessitate unanimity. For although, ideally, when God is guiding one, he will be guiding all, in practice the receiving of guidance is not that simple. As a result, there are occasions when there are some who see things differently.

The question then arises: What do we do if we see things differently? What are the options open to us if, after having conscientiously sought the mind of Christ, we find ourselves in the minority on a particular issue?

The first option is to accept the decision of the church meeting as an expression of God's will. From a theological perspective God speaks not just though those who have contributed to the discussion in the church meeting, but also in the actual decision that members have prayerfully made. In church meetings we come together in the name of Jesus, and when we do so, he has promised to be present (Matthew 18:20). To oppose the decision of a church meeting can be tantamount to opposing the Lord Jesus himself. The fact is that none of us has a monopoly on the Holy Spirit. All of us are fallible. At the time we may well have believed we were right, but on reflection we realize that perhaps we were wrong.

Alternatively, although we may still see the strength of our original position, we are prepared to recognize that the majority of our brothers and sisters have seen things otherwise, and so we accept the decision of the majority and move forward accordingly. In theological terms, the church has tested the spirits (see 1 John 4:1) and the church has been led to make its decision. Who are we to quarrel with the leading of the Spirit?

Just occasionally, however, the situation may arise when in all conscience we struggle to accept the decision of the church meeting. Although God appears to have spoken clearly to his church as a whole, we ourselves find it impossible to hear him speaking in the decision that has been made. What then are we to do?

One possible way forward is to follow the example of Gamaliel. For although Gamaliel in all conscience could not respond positively to the preaching of Peter and John, he strongly advised his fellow Jews not to oppose the new preaching. Instead, he told them to wait and see: 'If what they have planned and done is of human origin, it will disappear, but if it comes from God, you cannot possibly defeat them. You could find yourselves fighting against God' (Acts 5:38–39).

But what if we cannot accept the Gamaliel option? Then, sadly, the only option left is surely to leave the church and find another church whose direction we can more happily accept. The fact is that a parting of the ways (see Acts 15:36–39) is always preferable to in-fighting in the church.[1]

Covenant renewal

After a period of difficulty within our church, we drew a line on the past by adopting the following covenant. We renew this covenant every September:

Lord Jesus, you are Lord of our lives and Lord of your church.
We will act in love toward one another.
We will care for one another.
We will support those you have called to lead us.
With your help we resolve to do our best to preserve the unity of your church.

Lord Jesus, you wish to enter the hearts and lives of everybody.
We will pray for those who have yet to respond to your love.
We will invite friends to come to our church.
We will make our church a place where strangers feel at home.
With your help we resolve to do our best to make disciples.

Scriptures to reflect on

- 'How very good and pleasant it is / when kindred live together in unity!' (Psalm 133:1).
- 'I ask . . . that they may become completely one, so that the world may know that you have sent me . . .'(John 17:20, 23).
- 'May the God of steadfastness and encouragement grant you to live in harmony with one another, in accordance with Christ Jesus, so that together you may with one voice glorify the God and Father of our Lord Jesus Christ' (Romans 15:5–6).
- 'I . . . beg you to lead a life worthy of the calling to which you have been called . . . making every effort to maintain the unity of the Spirit in the bond of peace' (Ephesians 4:1, 3).
- 'Live your life in a manner worthy of the gospel of Christ . . . standing firm in one spirit, striving side by side with one mind for the faith of the gospel' (Philippians 1:27).

11. Exercise church discipline

Church discipline is one of those things that most, if not all, ministers would rather avoid. And yet there are times when discipline is essential to the health of the church. 'Without discipline', said John Calvin, 'the church is like a body without sinews.' Indeed, the Reformers used to consider the exercise of discipline as one of essential marks of a true church. Similarly, one of our leading Anabaptist forefathers, Balthasar Hubmaier, wrote: 'Where church discipline is lacking, there is certainly no church, even if Baptism and the Supper of Christ are practised.'

So how do we go about it? How do we put into practice today the teaching of Jesus as found in Matthew 18:15–17 as also the teaching of Paul found in Galatians 6:1–3?

In the first place, we need to recognize that discipline is a form of pastoral care, which always has the good of the individual(s) in mind. It is, in fact, a form of loving. Just as in a family children need to experience both encouragement and correction if they are to grow up to maturity, so too in the Christian life we all need to experience from one another both encouragement and correction. Discipline in this sense is not a big deal – but rather just part and parcel of the way we relate to one another.

But, there are times, when the church and its leaders have to get involved. In this respect perhaps the following guidelines might be of help.

Leaders have a responsibility for safeguarding the spiritual health of the church, which from time to time may involve exercising church discipline. The purpose of church discipline is to bring back a person to the Lord: restoration and not punishment is the aim. Specific help and support needs to be offered to the 'offending' person. Church discipline needs to be concerned for every aspect of the Christian life, and not just for sexual or financial misdemeanours.

Church discipline in the first instance normally involves private pastoral visits by church leaders to individuals who are judged to be at fault. Only in exceptional circumstances, where the discipline of the leaders is rejected, should the names of church members be brought to the church meeting with a view to their suspension or removal from the church roll.

Where suspension or removal from the church roll is in view, the offending member needs to be asked to refrain from taking communion, for the Lord's Table is not 'open to all those who love our Lord Jesus Christ' without condition; rather, it is open only to those who 'truly and earnestly repent of their sins and are in love and charity with their neighbours'.

Church discipline is a responsibility delegated by the church to its leaders. Therefore, on those occasions when a name is brought to the church meeting, church members should not normally be given an opportunity to express their opinion on the disciplinary action that has been taken. To embark on such a discussion would inevitably involve the leadership sharing further details, which would in turn yet further undermine people's character.[1]

Be clear about the principles of church discipline

In the New Testament, church discipline is not a forerunner of the horrors perpetrated in the Spanish inquisition, but an expression of brotherly or sisterly love. Indeed, the Anabaptists used to talk of 'the authority of fraternal admonition'. So in response to the question 'But what right has one brother to use this authority on another?', Balthasar Hubmaier's catechism stated: 'From the baptismal pledge in which a man subjects himself to the church and to all her members according to the word of Christ.'[2]

This understanding of discipline as a mark of love is expressed by Paul when he equated the bearing of one another's burdens with caring for those who fail:

> My friends, if anyone is detected in a transgression, you who have received the Spirit should restore such a one in a spirit of gentleness. Take care that you yourselves are not tempted. Bear one another's burdens, and in this way you will fulfil the law of Christ.
> (Galatians 6:1–2)

Here we discover four important principles for caring for those who fail.

First, church discipline is no optional extra. 'If someone is caught in any kind of wrong-doing' (Good News Bible), then action is necessary (see Matthew 18:15, where some manuscripts omit the words 'against you'). We are responsible for one another. We cannot simply ignore sin, for sin brings the church into disrepute and spoils the witness of the church. Furthermore, like a nasty virus, sin can spread and damage others. 'If they can get away with it, why can't I?' Perhaps more importantly, sin can permanently damage the persons involved. Unless action is taken, they can be lost to the Christian faith altogether. Sadly all too often churches don't take action. They turn a blind eye. It's all so embarrassing! And if they do take action, it is left until too late. Church discipline exercised in such a way is tantamount to the last rites!

Secondly, church discipline has restoration, and not punishment, as its aim. The underlying Greek verb (*katartizō*), translated as 'restore' or 'set right', connotes remedial action and literally means 'to return to an original state', 'to reconstruct something broken down'. It was used in secular Greek as a medical term for setting a fractured or dislocated bone; and is found in Mark 1:19 to describe James and John 'mending' their nets. In other words, discipline is a positive action, which has the welfare of the individual at heart. We are trying to bring a person back to the Lord, not send him or her packing. The presumption here is that the individual concerned will respond positively to the help offered. Sadly, there are occasions when individuals respond negatively; when in spite of the exposure of their sin, they refuse to be penitent. Ultimately, a church may be left with no choice but to exclude the person from their membership (see Matthew 18:17). Yet even exclusion should not be seen as the last word.

Thirdly, church discipline must never be exercised heavy-handedly, but rather 'in a gentle way'. Gentleness (rendered by the Good News Bible as 'humility') is a fruit of the Spirit (see Galatians 5:22–23). Gentleness does not rule out firmness. There is a time when a Christian has to tell another: 'What you have done is wrong.' There is a time when love requires confrontation. Not to confront can be the opposite of loving. But there is no place for carpeting a brother or sister in Christ. The odds are that he or she already feels pretty guilty – it is not for us to turn the screw even more. In the words of Luther, 'Run unto him, and reaching out your hand, raise him up again, comfort him with sweet words, and embrace him with motherly arms.'[3]

Fourthly, church discipline needs to be exercised humbly, for the fact is that we are all fallible: 'take care that you yourselves are not tempted'. There is no room for judgmentalism or false pride of any kind (see Luke 18:11). As Jesus once said, it is only the person without sin who may throw the first stone (John 8:8)!

Scriptures to reflect on
- 'If another member of the church sins against you, go and point out the fault when the two of you are alone. If the member listens to you, you have regained that one ...' (Matthew 18:15).
- 'If another disciple sins, you must rebuke the offender, and if there is repentance, you must forgive' (Luke 17:3).
- 'When you are assembled ... you are to hand this man [who is 'living with his father's wife'] over to Satan ... so that his spirit may be saved in the day of the Lord' (1 Corinthians 5:4–5).
- 'If you think you are standing, watch out that you do not fall' (1 Corinthians 10:12).
- 'Whoever brings back a sinner from wandering will save the sinner's soul from death and will cover a multitude of sins' (James 5:19–20).

12. Revise the church roll regularly

Roll revision is a task in which every church should engage, ideally annually. However, the temptation is to put off the task with the result that church rolls often list a number of people who may be 'in membership' but are not actually 'in fellowship'. This is a nonsense.

Painful though it may be, roll revision is good for the church. It encourages integrity – it just isn't honest for a church in its annual returns to the Baptist Union to claim more members than it actually has attending the church. It encourages commitment – it is difficult to urge people to take their membership responsibilities seriously when there are members who have not attended the church for several years! It also encourages growth – growing churches for the most part are churches with high commitment, where 'membership is not viewed as a destination, but rather as a pilgrimage that leads one towards unreserved discipleship and a higher level of religious commitment'.[1]

But how in practice do we go about revising the roll? There was a stage in the life of our church when we had to engage in some fairly substantial roll revision. Before we set about the task, we agreed the following 'non-rigorist' guidelines.

First of all, when members move out of the area, they will be encouraged to link up with another church as soon as possible. If no request for a transfer or commendation has come through within six months, the pastoral deacon will write or telephone with a view to yet again encouraging the process of commitment to another church. Once members have left the area for more than a period of twelve months, their membership will normally lapse.

Secondly, when members living in the area do not attend our church at all in a twelve-month period, they will be visited, and unless there is some good reason (e.g. ill health or old age), their membership will lapse. However, their names will be retained in the church handbook in the category of friends for a further period of two years, after which the matter will be reviewed.

These guidelines are 'non-rigorist' in the sense that they are far less draconian than those adopted by some churches. As a teenager, for instance, I belonged to a Baptist church were (in theory at least) if you had not attended a communion service for three months, you would be visited by a deacon; and if you had not attended for six months, your name would automatically be deleted from the membership roll (those were the days when members had to put into the offering bag their communion tickets – in this way absences could be duly noted!).

Needless to say: when we prune the roll, we hope that the process will result not in the deletion of a name, but in restoration to fellowship. Yes, roll revision is painful, and yet (in the words of Jesus' parable of the vine) a branch is pruned 'to make it bear more fruit' (John 15:2).[2]

Membership is about commitment

Talk of church membership is confusing to people who attend state churches (e.g. the Church of England) where in the past the assumption has been that everybody belongs to the local parish church unless they have opted out. Indeed, this assumption is still present in the thinking of many Anglican priests who appear to understand the term 'parish' more in geographical as distinct from people terms. Even if that underlying assumption is not always true, it is still difficult to know what membership means in an Anglican church. Is it someone who has been baptized, or is confirmation a necessary adjunct? Or is membership of an Anglican church to be equated with registration on the parish electoral roll or attendance at Easter communion?

By contrast, in most other denominations there is normally no room for doubt as to who belongs. A member is someone who has been admitted to the church roll and who in one way or another now has some kind of responsibility for the life of the church. For instance, in Baptist as also in Congregational way of thinking the church is viewed as a community of believers gathered together out of the world, who have committed themselves to Christ and to one another.

Church membership in these terms is not just about being a name on a roll. It is about living together in community. I often say that it gives us the right, where necessary, to knock one another up at midnight and ask for help (see Luke 11:5–8), or at least that is the theory. Church membership is a high privilege.

Although social patterns in the church today are different from social patterns in the early church, it is clear that the early church had distinct and definite boundaries. People knew whether they were in or out of the church. For instance, Matthew records that, in the context of the brother or sister who sins and then refuses to heed the admonition of fellow Christians, Jesus said: 'If the member refuses to listen to them, tell it to the church; and if the offender refuses to listen even to the church, let such a one be to you as a Gentile and a tax-collector' (Matthew 18:17). Church discipline cannot be exercised where people are not in a committed relationship. Church discipline can only work where there is a clear sense of church membership. Church membership, then and now, is about committed relationships.

Inevitably (for we are dealing with fallen men and women), there are times when things go wrong and hopes and dreams fail to materialize, with the result that not all those whom we welcome into membership stay the course. The reasons for this vary. Sometimes the fault may lie in the new members themselves – like Demas of old they fall 'in love with this present world' (2 Timothy 4:10) and therefore leave the church. More often the fault lies with the church itself. We fail to keep our promise 'to love, encourage, pray for and care for' those who commit themselves to church membership. In our life together there is often disagreement and difference, even conflict and power struggles, with the result that people become disillusioned, if not deeply hurt, and leave the church. Whatever, for one reason or another, people leave. And what then? Ideally, at some stage the church roll needs to be revised. But how? Some churches, instead of striking people off the membership roll, have an annual self-selecting procedure. On this model they automatically disband the church membership every year and people are invited to re-enrol, say at the first communion service of the New Year. By contrast many other churches take little or no action whatever, with the result that their church membership rolls are wildly unrealistic. My own preference is the somewhat non-rigorist approach expounded in my original article.

Scriptures to reflect on

- 'Other seed fell on rocky ground . . . and . . . withered away. Other seed fell among thorns, and the thorns grew up and choked it' (Mark 4:5, 7).
- The vine-grower 'removes every branch in me that bears not fruit. Every branch that bears fruit he prunes to make it bear more fruit' (John 15:2).
- 'Do you show contempt for the church of God?' (1 Corinthians 11:22).
- 'Godly grief produces a repentance that leads to salvation' (2 Corinthians 7:10).
- 'Demas, in love with this present world, has deserted me' (2 Timothy 4:10).

13. Liven up the AGM

I hate AGMs – there is nothing more boring than listening to annual reports and adopting annual accounts. What's more, how an earth can we reconcile an AGM with the church meeting's stated desire of 'submitting ourselves to the guidance of the Holy Spirit and standing under the judgment of God that we may know the mind of Christ'?

Technically, maybe a Baptist church meeting could dispense with an AGM, for in the eyes of the law it is the ministers and deacons who are the trustees of the church, so presumably the AGM could become the preserve of the ministers and deacons. However, the reality is that all Baptist churches need an occasion when (at the very least) the annual accounts are adopted, the church officers are reappointed and annual reports are given. So, faced with this reality, how do we overcome the boredom factor?

A number of suggestions come to mind.

First of all, every AGM needs to take place within the context of worship (for at an AGM we come above all to thank God for all his goodness over the past year. The emphasis needs to be not on what we have done, but on what God has done through his people) and praise him accordingly. This does not mean that we do not recognize the time and effort people have given. Far from it – an AGM is a place for cheers as well as praise.

Secondly, to ensure that the meeting is not overwhelmed by a multiplicity of reports from the various organizations and activities, there is a lot to be said for all reports being brought together in a booklet and distributed prior to the meeting – on the understanding that members will indeed bother to read the reports. The minister or the church treasurer might still want to highlight certain aspects of reports, but hopefully this can be done visually (if not using PowerPoint, then at least using an OHP) rather than verbally.

Thirdly, although detailed church accounts should always be available to those who want to see them, the presentation of the accounts should be restricted to basic headlines. There is no reason why church members should, for instance, know how much was spent on toilet rolls in the past year (for the record, this is not an exaggeration: I was actually present at a church meeting when the treasurer was asked to account for the church's expenditure on toilet rolls!).

Fourthly, the AGM provides an opportunity for the church to look forward. This is the moment when the leaders of the church cast the vision for the coming twelve months. AGMs are a place for the church to engage in possibility-thinking as the members reflect on what God might be calling them to do.

Fifthly, AGMs can be an excuse for eating and drinking together. The business might be done more quickly if members know that at the end there will be coffee and cake for everybody. Better still, why not bring out some sparkling white and celebrate the goodness of God in style? (Confession: this last idea I have yet to put into practice!)

AGMs can be occasions to be looked forward to![1]

I believe in the church

I readily confess an impatience with some of the more 'bureaucratic' aspects of the church's life. The formalities of an AGM, although necessary, do not appeal to me. But nonetheless, I passionately believe in the church, and in the local church in particular. At the end of the day 'translocal' ministries (whether they be para-church or denominational) are there only to serve the needs of the local church. There is no higher calling than of being pastor of a local church.

It is out of this passionate belief in the local church that I developed the following 'confession of faith' in the church:

> I believe in the church. Indeed, at the heart of my calling to be your minister is a passion to enable our church to *be* church. I am saddened that in so many places the church is a stumbling block to Christian faith. I want to be a minister of a church whose very life is a powerful testimony to the gospel.
>
> I believe that the church is the temple of the Spirit (1 Corinthians 3:16), and as such it is to be the place where God makes himself known. One of the challenges your ministers face week by week is to lead the worship and preach in such a way that the worship and the preaching prove to be a vehicle for God's Spirit.
>
> I believe that the church is the bride of Christ, and as such is called to be radiant with the beauty of holiness (Ephesians 5:26). Another of the challenges your ministers face, not only on a Sunday but also in their pastoral work, is to promote that kind of attractive holiness.
>
> I believe that the church is the body of Christ, and as such is called to be a community where relationships are paramount (1 Corinthians 12:12). In this respect, another of the challenges your ministers face is to promote 'body ministry', encouraging all to discover their gifts and to play their part.
>
> I believe in the church as the people of God gathered in one place. My understanding of Scripture is that the church of God is always local (e.g. 1 Corinthians 1:2) and only by extension, universal. The local church is the cutting edge of the kingdom of God. What a privilege; what a responsibility!
>
> Because I believe in the church, I believe in church membership. Indeed, the New Testament makes it clear that church membership is not an option for those who believe in the Lord Jesus Christ. Commitment to Christ inevitably involves commitment to the people of Christ, and this commitment is expressed through church membership. Because I believe in the local church, commitment to Christ is in the first place expressed through membership of a local church. This has all

kinds of implications. For instance, it means that the level of our commitment to Christ is reflected in the level of our commitment to Christ's people. The degree to which I love the Lord Jesus is the degree to which I love my brothers and sisters (see John 13:34–35). I find it difficult to understand how people can ever think of resigning from church membership (as distinct from transferring to another church). Theologically speaking, to resign is tantamount to giving up on Christ!

Because I believe in the church, I believe in the church meeting (see Acts 15). In the Baptist understanding of the church, the church meeting is the place where we express our commitment to Christ and to one another. The church meeting is not simply the place where we discern the mind of Christ – it is also the place where the body of Christ comes to expression. From where then did the idea come that the church meeting is in the first place a business meeting?

Because I believe in the church, I believe in church discipline (Matthew 18:15–20). The Reformers in general, and our spiritual forebears in particular, taught that for a church to be a church there must be the preaching of the word, the administration of the sacraments, and the exercise of church discipline. A church without discipline is like a body without sinews. It is to our detriment that church discipline has become an abnormal part of the church's life!

Because I believe in the church, I believe in church leadership (Acts 6:1–7). The Scriptures teach that God calls some to serve his church through leading his church forward in mission and ministry. A church without leadership is a church that is going nowhere. Of course, leaders are fallible, but with all their warts they are Christ's gift to his church and as such are to be valued – and therefore encouraged.

Because I believe in the church, I believe in church growth (Matthew 16:13–20). In particular, I believe that Jesus wants to build his church here – not just through transfer growth, but above all through conversion growth. I long to see people won for Christ and his church. I long to see God's Spirit touch us all in such a way that we truly become 'contagious Christians'.

Scriptures to reflect on
- 'I will build my church' (Matthew 16:18).
- 'You are God's temple ... God's Spirit dwells in you'
  (1 Corinthians 3:16).
- 'All things should be done decently and in order' (1 Corinthians
  14:40).
- 'Christ loved the church and gave himself up for her, in order
  to make her holy by cleansing her with the washing of water
  by the word, so as to present the church to himself in
  splendour, without a spot or wrinkle or anything of the kind'
  (Ephesians 5:25–27).
- 'Like living stones, let yourselves be built into a spiritual
  house' (1 Peter 2:5).

Part 3: Pastoral care
14. Structure pastoral care

Although pastoral care is the responsibility of us all (see 1 Corinthians 12:25), any responsible church will appoint people with a specific responsibility for the care of its members.

It varies from church to church as to who exactly makes up this group. In my own church, in addition to a pastoral team, we have a larger group of care-group leaders responsible for the various care groups into which the church is divided. Their task is simple: to love those in their care. However, to make the task clearer, we devised the following guidelines.

First, in a church as large as ours it is very easy for people to feel lost and uncared for. Your primary task is to ensure that all those within your group feel loved, wanted and cared for; in a sense you represent the Lord and his love to all those in your care. To keep track of people in your care group, you may find it helpful to have an informal register, in which you mark absences from church!

A secondary role is to be the eyes and ears of the ministers and the pastoral team. Please inform us of concerns: for example, sickness, loneliness, loss of faith, family problems, redundancy and so on.

Eight practical ways of fulfilling your caring role: (1) Share the caring with others in the group, and in this way practice 'one-anotherness'.

(2) Pray for members of your group – and encourage them to pray for one another. Consider establishing a telephone 'prayer chain', where you alert each other to pray for special needs. (3) Visit all the housebound members of your group, and ensure that they are visited regularly (fortnightly?) by someone in the group. (4) Encourage those in your care on a regular basis. Aim to have a monthly 'pastoral conversation' with every member of the group. Remember that pastoral care is helping people not just to cope with life's crises, but also to grow in the faith. Feel free to lend a good Christian book you have just read, or to suggest a series of Bible reading aids. (5) Recognize anniversaries. Make a list not just of birthdays and wedding anniversaries, but find out too when people were widowed. (6) Practise hospitality. Encourage members of the group to invite each other to their homes for a meal or for a cup of coffee. Maybe you might set a lead by having people in your home on a regular (monthly?) basis. (7) Organize social activities. Hold a party; for example, with other care groups in your area. (8) Offer practical help; for example, babysitting, transport, shopping, collecting library books, or help with housework, repairs, decorating and so on.

These guidelines are very basic, but that is pastoral care![1]

Pastoral care at every level

The essence of pastoral care is loving one another. It is the fulfilling of the 'new commandment'. Pastoral care in this sense is the responsibility of every Christian. For this reason every time we welcome new members into our church, the congregation promises to 'love, encourage, pray for, and care for' them.

To help people care for one another we have produced a church handbook with the names and addresses of everybody associated with our church. The only difference between 'members', who have formally committed themselves to the church, and 'friends' is that the former have a special 'asterisk' (*) after their name. Most of the friends are members of the congregation. We also include the names of spouses, whether or not they attend church. In addition, we include the names of all the children of every church family, whether or not they still come to church. However, where children no longer come to church, once they reach the age of 18 their names are removed. To help us in our pastoral care, after the name of each child, we list the month and year of their birth (e.g. 12/04).

Another aid to pastoral care are our 'yellow cards' (15 cm × 10 cm) which are inserted into hymnbooks, and which are also available at the 'reception desk'. On one side of the card is space for visitors to make themselves known to us, and to tell us what they first noticed, and what they liked best! On the other side is space for regulars to give news and to let the ministers know of people in need of particular help. At every service mention is made of these cards and everybody is invited to fill them in. As a result, these cards form the agenda for much of the pastoral work of the church.

Although all Christians have a duty to care for their brothers and sisters, some are more gifted than others in exercising pastoral care. It makes sense to recognize those with such gifts by forming them into a pastoral team. A key task of the minister is then to give support to the team members, meeting with them regularly and together sharing news and concerns.

In our setting we have two levels of caring: a large group of caregivers with whom I meet on a termly basis, and a smaller pastoral team with whom I meet on a six-weekly basis. At least once a term we offer training to all involved in pastoral care, when we have had talks about autism, depression, disability, ME, mental illness, the needs of older people, the needs of younger people, as also caring in a multicultural situation and caring for 'problem' people.

Pastoral care, of course, is not just about caring for people with 'needs'. It is also about encouraging and enabling people to grow and develop in their spiritual walk. So we reflect together too on how we can be 'soul-friends' and not just 'carers'.

It is only within this context of general care that we can talk of the role ministers have to play. One of the key ministerial roles is to support their leaders; yet another is to visit newcomers and help them integrate into the church. Then there is the 'bread and butter' work associated with the rites of passage (weddings, funerals, dedications, baptisms) as also the visiting of the hospitalized and people in special need.

Although every minister is involved in counselling of one kind or another, there is a difference between a minister and a counsellor. Crudely put, the pastor seeks to encourage people to grow in

Christ, while the counsellor seeks to enable people to reach self-understanding. The pastor may through prayer bring God and his grace into the situation, while the counsellor aims to release resources from within. The pastor is free to initiate a pastoral conversation, but the counsellor is only free to respond to a request for counselling. The pastor may be dealing with people on a one-off basis, while the counsellor rarely sees people for fewer than six sessions. The pastor will often be dealing with people whom he sees in other church and social contexts, but the counsellor keeps at a distance and sees only clients.

Pastoral care does indeed take place at many levels.

Scriptures to reflect on
- 'I will seek the lost, and I will bring back the strayed, and I will bind up the injured, and I will strengthen the weak ... ' (Ezekiel 34:16).
- 'When he saw the crowds, he had compassion for them, because they were harassed and helpless, like sheep without a shepherd' (Matthew 9:36).
- 'Feed my lambs ... Feed my sheep' (John 21:15, 17).
- 'It is he [Christ] whom we proclaim, warning everyone and teaching everyone in all wisdom, so that we may present everyone mature in Christ' (Colossians 1:28).
- 'We dealt with each one of you like a father with his children, urging and encouraging you and pleading that you should lead a life worthy of God' (1 Thessalonians 2:11–12).

15. Bring God into life's special occasions

Earlier this year two of our church members asked me to conduct a service of thanksgiving on the occasion of their golden wedding prior to a celebratory lunch. There were hymns – the couple had chosen 'Now thank we all our God' and 'Lord for the years your love has kept and guided'. There were Scripture readings (Psalm 121, a psalm of pilgrimage, and 1 Corinthians 13, the so-called hymn to love) together with an amusing Frank Topping extract, all read by family members; as also prayers led by the family. And of course, there was a brief address in which we reflected on how in all the ups and downs of the last fifty years God had been with them. In this respect I had asked the couple to sum up their life together within the compass of a sheet of A4.

The service came to a close as the congregation together recited Numbers 6:24–26 as a blessing on the couple. It was a great occasion, with a wide cross-section of family and friends in attendance. Many of those present were committed Christians, but others were not. And of those who were not, all without exception were deeply impressed by the way in which the service linked this couple's faith with the realities of everyday life. Would that I were given more opportunities to bring God into family life.

In this respect I remember hosting a meeting for ministers when the subject of anniversaries came up. We were acknowledging that one of the great privileges ministers have is being invited to events at which special milestones in the lives of families or individuals belonging to our church family are being celebrated. Yet at the same time we were expressing our surprise, as also our sadness, that all too often we are not called upon to say a word or to read a Scripture or to pray on such an occasion. Why is it, we wondered, that many Christian people seem to forget to bring God into a party? Surely, nothing should be more natural than to thank God for his goodness in the past, and to pray for God's blessing in the future. It would give any minister the greatest of pleasures to pray for and rejoice with friends in this way. Perhaps we ministers are in part to blame. Maybe we should be more proactive and actually offer our services.

On reflection, it's not simply anniversaries or special birthdays where we ministers would love to be involved. There are all kinds of other 'rites of passage' where we ministers can be used: it might be an engagement party or a retirement celebration, a house-warming or a farewell party for a child leaving home for university. Or it might not be a 'rite of passage' at all: it could be a fundraising lunch or a simple supper party, where all that might be appropriate is for the minister to be asked to say grace. As a minister I have always been grateful for the opportunity to bring God into family life. What's more, it always leads into all kinds of conversations about the Christian faith.[1]

A service of thanksgiving on the occasion of a golden wedding
Introduction: 'Your lips cover me with kisses; your love is better
                than wine ... Take me with you, and we'll run away;
                be my king and take me to your room. We will be
                happy together, drink deep, and lose ourselves in
                love' (Song of Songs 1:2, 4, Good News Bible). 'Every
                good gift and every perfect present comes from ...
                God, the Creator' (James 1:16, Good News Bible).
                   On this day of celebration let me turn your
                attention to two verses from the book of
                Lamentations, which affirm that amidst all the ups
                and downs of life, God can be relied upon: 'the

steadfast love of the Lord never ceases, / his mercies never come to an end; / they are new every morning; / great is your faithfulness' (Lamentations 3:22–23).

HYMN: 'Now thank we all our God'.

Prayer: Father God, together with ... and ..., many of us not only want to thank you for the good things in their marriage, but also in ours. Yes, Lord, those of us who are married, or indeed have been married, thank you for all the fun and laughter we have known, for those quieter moments of deepening companionship, as also for the secret intimacies of our lovemaking. We thank you for all that we have had in common, and also for those differing interests and differing insights which have broadened our life together.

We thank you for the homes that we have been able to make, and for the children with which many of us have been blessed. We thank you for all the good times we have been through together, and for all that we have learnt together in the bad times too. We thank you for friends who have enriched our lives, as also for friends who have stood by us in difficult days. Above all we thank you for the difference you have made to our lives: giving us purpose and direction, helping us to cope when life has been tough, and deepening our joy when life has been good. For all these gifts of your grace, we thank you.

And yet, along with our thanksgiving, we come to seek your forgiveness. For all of us have, in one way or another, failed you and failed one another. We have not always loved as you would have us love. Father, forgive us for the times when we have hurt one another; when we have shown lack of respect and lack of understanding for one another; when we have fought with one another rather than prayed for one another. Forgive us for the many ways in which we have spoiled that perfect relationship you planned for us together. For the for sake of your Son Jesus Christ, forgive us for all that is past; and by the power of your Holy Spirit help us to live more truly lives that are well pleasing in your sight.

Scriptures: Psalm 121 (*The Message*) and 1 Corinthians 13.

Address: Mark Twain said: 'No man or woman knows what perfect love is until they have been married a quarter of a century.' But you have been married half a century. That is some achievement!

What is the secret of a long, happy marriage? According to Agatha Christie, it was being married to an archaeologist: 'An archaeologist is the best husband any woman can have – the older she gets, the more interested he is in her.' According to the Christian psychotherapist, Anne Townsend, the willingness to forgive is the key to a long, happy marriage: 'Forgiveness of oneself and of one's partner can be the secret source of strength, enabling a marriage to survive.' It has been said that 'marriage is three parts love and seven parts forgiveness' (Langdon Mitchell). 'Love', said Paul, 'does not keep a record of wrongs . . . Love never gives up' (1 Corinthians 13:5, 7, Good News Bible).

I want to suggest that God is the one who above all makes the difference. In the words of the Preacher: 'A rope made up of three cords is hard to break' (Ecclesiastes 4:12, Good News Bible).

I am so glad that you chose Psalm 121, a psalm sung by pilgrims as they journeyed to Jerusalem. 'I look up to the mountains; / does my strength come from the mountains?' (Good News Bible). No, the very reverse. The mountains for the pilgrims of old symbolized danger: they were the hiding places of wild beasts and of robbers; they were also places where a stumble could lead to a plunge to death.

'Does my strength come from the mountains? No, my strength comes from God, who made heaven, earth and mountains.'

In your life together you have known all kinds of ups and downs. What a difference God makes. For although God does not promise us a life free from trouble, he does promise that he will be with us in our troubles – and that he won't allow those troubles to overwhelm us. In the words of the psalmist: 'He won't let you stumble; your Guardian God won't fall asleep. Not on your life! He will never doze or sleep.'

God is the great insomniac: he never goes off-duty; he stays awake, working on our behalf. The psalmist concludes: 'He guards you when you leave and when you return, he guards you now, he guards you always.' He is there at every stage of life – he was there when fifty years ago you set off on life's journey together – he will be there at the end of life's journey too. So today you can look forward to the future with confidence, for God is with you in all your journeyings.

Prayers: We ask God's blessing on the couple.

HYMN: 'Lord, for the years your love has kept and guided'.

The Blessing: Numbers 6:24–26.

Scriptures to reflect on
- 'For everything there is a season' (Ecclesiastes 3:1).
- 'A threefold cord is not quickly broken' (Ecclesiastes 4:12).
- 'The water . . . had become wine' (John 2:9).
- 'I am the resurrection and the life' (John 11:25).
- 'I can do all things through him who strengthens me' (Philippians 4:13).

16. Encourage cohabitees to marry

Today cohabitation is the norm – most couples live together before they marry. Although a good number of these relationships are unstable, some undoubtedly involve the kind of commitment that one would desire for any married couple. As a result, there is a tendency to equate such committed relationships with the marriage relationship itself. And yet it is not the same.

Marriage involves the making of lifelong vows – 'till death do us part'; while cohabitation is a present relationship where the future is ill-defined. Furthermore, marriage is a public act in which families as also the community in general are involved (indeed, the law requires that the doors of the church have to be open during a wedding!), while cohabitation tends to be a private relationship between two individuals.

I see cohabiting couples as couples on the way to marriage – although perhaps 'betrothed' to one another, they have yet fully to 'cleave' to one another. Although they may enjoy sexual union, I do not see a cohabiting couple as being truly 'one flesh' – sexual intercourse is an integral part of marriage (indeed, in law a marriage without sexual union is not a marriage and can therefore be annulled), but by itself it does not make a marriage.

Like most ministers, I find that most of the couples I marry are already living together. This causes me no problem when the couple concerned are not members of my church. In my initial interview with them, I tell them quite openly that as a Christian minister I cannot approve of their living arrangements; but I go on to say that I am more than happy to marry them and in that way 'regularize' their present relationship.

For me the issue of cohabitation becomes a pastoral problem when the couple concerned are church members. For my reading of Scripture is that when a couple live together without committing themselves in marriage, then they are going against the clear teaching of Scripture. This being so, as a Christian minister I cannot allow such a situation to continue without the exercise of some form of 'church discipline'.

Some time ago I faced this problem with two young members who began to live together before their wedding day. As we talked through the issue, they realized the error of their ways. So on the night before their wedding day we held a private service of penitence in which they acknowledged they had 'sinned by following the way of the world, living together without first seeking God's blessing upon our relationship together'. But at the same time I along with my two ministerial colleagues confessed before them that 'we too are in need of God's grace and his forgiveness; for we too have sinned in thought and word and deed'. In other words, we were recognizing that in our varying ways all of us had things that needed to be put right; all of us 'live in sin', whether or not we cohabit. This mutual recognition, however, does not do away with the need for church discipline. There are things that are right, and things that are wrong. And as a church we need to make a stand on all these issues.[1]

A service of confession and of blessing

Words of assurance

Jesus said: 'There will be more joy in heaven over one sinner who repents than over ninety-nine righteous people who do not need to repent' (Luke 15:7). Paul said: 'This is a true saying, to be completely accepted and believed: Christ Jesus came into the world to save sinners' (1 Timothy 1:15, Good News Bible). John wrote: 'If we confess our sins to God, he will keep his promise and do what is right: he will forgive us our sins and purify us from all wrong-doing' (1 John 1:9, Good News Bible).

The invitation

Jesus also said: 'Where two or three come together in my name, I am there with them' (Matthew 18:20, Good News Bible). It is in the name of Jesus that we meet together this evening. Jesus is present with us – Jesus, who looks on our sorrow and hears our prayer. Therefore let us open our hearts to him and confess our sins, confident in his great mercy.

Confession

The couple: We confess to almighty God, and before you our brothers, that we have sinned by following the way of the world, living together without first seeking God's blessing upon our relationship together. For this and all other sins we pray for God's grace and ask his forgiveness.

The ministers: We confess to almighty God that we too are in need of God's grace and his forgiveness; for we too have sinned in thought and word and deed.

Together: Father God, for the sake of Jesus, your Son, who died for us, forgive us for all that is past; and by the power of the Spirit, by which you raised Jesus from death, grant that we may serve you in newness of life; to the glory of your name. Amen.

The absolution and blessing

To all who confess their sins and resolve to lead a new life, Jesus says: 'Your sins are forgiven.' So let us receive his pardon and experience his peace.

And may the blessing of God Almighty, Father, Son and Holy Spirit, be upon us today, and in all the days that lie ahead.

Extempore prayer

For the
- wedding day
- future

The Grace
Together: The grace of our Lord Jesus Christ, the love of God, and the fellowship of the Holy Spirit, be upon us all, evermore. Amen

Scriptures to reflect on
- 'Two are better than one' (Ecclesiastes 4:9).
- 'Set me as a seal upon your heart' (Song of Songs 8:6).
- 'From the beginning of creation, "God made them male and female." For this reason a man shall leave his father and mother and be joined to his wife, and the two shall become one flesh' (Mark 10:6–8).
- 'It is better to marry than to be aflame with passion' (1 Corinthians 7:9).
- 'Husbands, love your wives, just as Christ loved the church and gave himself up for her' (Ephesians 5:25).

17. Marry divorcees

On this vexed and painful issue, let's start with what the Bible teaches. Although marriage is clearly intended for life, the Bible recognizes that, since the fall, human beings have lived life on a less than ideal level. Deuteronomy 24:1–4 therefore allows divorce on the grounds of 'uncleanness' – Jews have long debated as to whether this included any inappropriate behaviour or just sexual infidelity. In the context of a society where women could be divorced without any rights, and often for trivial reasons, Jesus upheld the permanent nature of marriage (see Matthew 19:5–6); he pointed out that divine permission for divorce had only been given because of human sinfulness (Matthew 19:8), and went on to say that 'whoever divorces his wife, except for unchastity, and marries another commits adultery' (Matthew 19:9; also 5:32).

It is a matter of scholarly debate whether the mention of adultery is an example of the sort of serious sin that merits a permissible divorce, or whether it is the unique exception. My own conviction is that by regarding adultery as the one and only ground for divorce, we may be in danger of falling into the kind of legalism that Jesus often condemned. For although Jesus clearly held a very high view of marriage, he also recognized that there are times when marriages do irretrievably break down, and went on to allow for the possibility of remarriage. Interestingly, Paul added a further permissible cause for divorce; namely, desertion by an unbelieving partner. In such circumstances he also allowed for the possibility of remarriage (1 Corinthians 7:12–16).

We also need to recognize that, beyond the immediate texts about marriage and divorce, the Scriptures contain much material relating to God's grace and forgiveness. Time and again the Bible makes clear that with God there is always a new beginning: the potter, for instance, can rework the clay (see Jeremiah 18)! Grace and not law has the last word.

For reasons such as these I am willing in principle to marry in church people who have been divorced. However, before I agree to go ahead with the wedding, there are a number of conditions I seek to ensure are met. Those wishing to be remarried need to recognize that through failing to be faithful to their original marriage vows they have failed both God as also their previous marriage partners. With few exceptions, there is no such thing as an 'innocent' party (as distinct from an 'injured' party). They need to be prepared to learn lessons from the failure of their previous marriage. It is unwise to enter a second marriage without personal growth and development. They need to be able to forgive (or at least seek to come to a place of forgiveness towards) their former partner, and not carry on a continuing vendetta. Where applicable, they need too to be dealing responsibly with the support of their previous partner and, especially, the children of the previous marriage. And, of course, above all, they need to be prepared to take seriously both God and his pattern for living.[1]

Jesus and divorce
In the UK almost four in ten marriages now end in divorce. There are many reasons for this. The position of women in society is very different today than what it used to be. In the past women had few rights, but now they stand on an equal footing to men. Patterns of employment have changed: wives as well as husbands go out to work, with the result that many wives are no longer financially dependent on their husbands. Furthermore, the provisions of the civil law make divorce much easier. Evidences of irretrievable breakdown are no longer limited to adultery, desertion and unreasonable behaviour;

they also include 'de facto' separation – two years if the couple agree to divorce, and five years if they do not. However, the greatest single reason for the massive growth in divorce is that attitudes to marriage have changed. Marriage in the minds of many is no longer about commitment, but about self-fulfilment. Married love is understood to be about getting, rather than giving, so that when difficulties come, as they inevitably do, it is all too easy to give up.

When Jesus was questioned about divorce, he made it clear that lifelong marriage is God's intention for us. In marriage there is no such thing as built-in obsolescence: 'What God has joined together, let no one separate' (Matthew 19:6).

From this it follows that divorce is always bad. There are not some good and bad divorces, depending on the circumstances. As far as Jesus is concerned, divorce is always an undoing of the work of God – it is the separating of what God has joined together.

One unfortunate result of the 1969 Divorce Reform Act is that by substituting the idea of 'irretrievable breakdown' for that of the 'matrimonial offence', it appeared to transfer the blame for any breakdown from the couple concerned to their marriage, as though the institution of marriage can be made into some kind of third-party scapegoat. But Jesus said: 'It was because you were so hard-hearted that Moses allowed you to divorce your wives' (Matthew 19:8); that is, Jesus traced the need for divorce to our hardness of heart, not to our incapacity to relate to one another. Divorce is always a sign of failure – a sign that we have failed God and one another.

However, although Jesus nowhere commended divorce, he did allow divorce. He acknowledged that the Scriptures gave permission for husbands to divorce their wives and he envisaged people remarrying (Matthew 19:8–9). From this we see that marriage is dissoluble. Although in marriage the two 'become one flesh' (Matthew 19:5), in certain circumstances the marriage bond can be undone.

The question arises: what are those circumstances? While Mark's Gospel suggests that there are no circumstances when divorce is possible (Mark 10:11–12), Matthew's Gospel contains an exception clause – 'except for unchastity' (verse 9). What does this mean? Jesus' hearers would have taken it for granted that divorce was allowable where there was adultery. In spite of their differences, both the school of Hillel and the school of Shammai accepted adultery as grounds for divorce. Did Jesus have in mind an unfaithfulness that went beyond adultery?

If we insist on adultery in the narrowest of senses, then we are falling foul of Pharisaical casuistry. What, I wonder, would Jesus say about day-to-day sadistic cruelty, selfishness, constant negative criticism and biting sarcasm? Cannot these sometimes be worse?

Jesus clearly set his face against easy divorce. Jesus would have those facing marriage difficulties explore every option possible before considering divorce – the services of a mediator and counsellor must always be sought before the services of a solicitor. Yet there are times when a marriage does break down, even if there has been no adultery.

One thing is for sure: Jesus' own acceptance of sinners suggests that people who go through the wrenching experience of divorce would receive from him forgiveness rather than condemnation. According to one tradition connected with the story of the woman caught in adultery, when Jesus stooped and began to write with his finger on the ground, he wrote the sins of which her accusers were guilty, and when they began to read words like pride, jealousy and hypocrisy, one by one they all slunk away. We are all sinners. A self-righteous hypocrite who goes regularly to church may be nearer hell than a generous-minded prostitute, let alone a victim of divorce.

Scriptures to reflect on
- 'A man leaves his father and his mother and clings to his wife, and they become one flesh' (Genesis 2:24).
- 'What God has joined together, let no one separate' (Matthew 19:6).
- 'Whoever divorces his wife, except for unchastity, and marries another commits adultery' (Matthew 19:9).
- 'Neither do I condemn you. Go your way, and from now on do not sin again' (John 8:11).
- 'If the unbelieving partner separates, let it be so; in such a case the brother or sister is not bound' (1 Corinthians 7:15).

18. Encourage a culture of forgiveness

November is a month for remembering. On 5 November we remember Guy Fawkes and his attempt to blow up the Houses of Parliament. On Remembrance Sunday we remember those who gave their lives in the service of our country. The first occasion for remembering is an opportunity for a bit of fun, but the second, for some at least, holds a degree of pain. This leads me on to ask the question: What do we do with painful memories?

As a pastor I know that there are many who continually wrestle with memories of failure. They find it difficult to believe that God is able to forgive all our sins and to remember them no more. But the good news is that when God forgives, he also forgets (see Isaiah 43:25).

Ideally, we too should be able to forgive and forget those who have failed us. However, there are times when it is well-nigh impossible to forget certain events, not least when, as a result of having been sinned against in one way or another, our lives have had to take a different direction. What then?

Clearly, the past cannot always be forgotten, but we can at least forgive those who have sinned against us and so ensure that the past no longer controls our hearts and our minds. Otherwise, bitterness develops, and where there is bitterness we are always the losers. Indeed, it is my experience as a pastor that unresolved anger and hurt all too often become displaced and transfer themselves in our feelings toward others, with the result that there is often a breakdown in present, as well as in past, relationships.

The fact is that even where the offending party has failed to see their need for forgiveness, for the sake of our own soul we must forgive, for otherwise our failure to let go of our anger and resentment will spoil not only our lives now but may well jeopardize even eternity itself (see Matthew 6:15).

One further thought. To 're-member' literally means putting back together something that has been broken and disconnected. This means more than recalling an event from the past – that is but a feat of memory. The opposite of remembering is not forgetting, but dismembering.

To truly remember requires that we turn back to past actions or relationships and recognize our own place within what happened – perhaps for the first time. As we begin to remember we may discover that far from having been totally in the right, we may actually have been in the wrong.

In that sense remembering can often be the key to restoring broken relationships. But for that to happen such remembering must go way beyond the nursing of old hurts and, instead, allow the hurts to be exposed in such a way that we discover our place in the cause of pain. Such remembering allows memories to become healing rather than destructive. Perhaps it was this kind of remembering that James had partly in mind when he urged his readers to 'confess your sins to one another, and pray for one another, so that you may be healed' (James 5:16).[1]

Finding strength to forgive

Forgiveness is a mark of a disciple of Jesus. Jesus taught his disciples to pray: 'And forgive us our debts, / as we also have forgiven our debtors' (Matthew 6:12). Augustine called this 'the terrible petition', terrible because of the condition attached – 'as we'. It is the only petition with a condition: God forgives only the forgiving.

This same need to forgive comes to expression on a number of occasions in the Gospels. 'Whenever you stand praying, forgive, if you have anything against anyone; so that your Father in heaven may also forgive you your trespasses' (Mark 11:25). Jesus also taught that the forgiveness of others was to be unlimited: even 'seventy times seven' (Matthew 18:22; see also Luke 17:3–4).

The teaching of Jesus is clear. Unfortunately, the putting of it into practice is not so easy, particularly where the offending party refuses to acknowledge that they have been at all in the wrong.

Many maintain that forgiveness is impossible where the offending party refuses to face up to the wrong they have done. However, a failure on the part of the offending party to see their need for forgiveness does not lessen the need to forgive. It makes it much more difficult, but does not make it impossible. One can indeed have the willingness to forgive or the spirit of forgiveness, regardless of the attitude of others. This willingness to forgive has sometimes been described as 'forgivingness' as over against 'forgiveness'. 'Forgivingness', where it meets with repentance, brings about forgiveness; but 'forgivingness' itself is not dependent on repentance.

One temptation Christians face is to deny the range of negative emotions that such perceived injustice inevitably arouses. Yet such denial actually makes true forgiveness impossible. For true forgiveness, far from suppressing, involves surfacing all that has been wrong; and then by God's grace letting go of the anger and resentment. Such a letting go is far from easy, especially in situations where the other people involved refuse to acknowledge any responsibility for their part in the tragedy. This refusal not only adds to the pain; it also prolongs the resolution of it. Yet forgive they must. For we are called to go the way of Christ, even the way of him who cried out: 'Father, forgive them; for they know not what they do' (Luke 23:34).

Forgiveness often takes time and tends to be a process. This process begins with a desire to forgive, but at least the desire to forgive is indicative of being on the right path.

For any victim, the process of forgiveness is painful and costly, just as it was for Christ. Feelings of anger and pain must be released before true forgiveness can ever be offered. But where such feelings of anger and pain are truly liberated, there the victim is liberated to live again. Strange as it may seem, the victim may eventually prove freer than the oppressor, because the oppressor is still caught up in a web of deceit and denial. The victim is free to grow and develop and go the way of Christ; the oppressor remains stuck on the journey, and instead of growing becomes twisted and stunted. Paradoxically, it is then the oppressor rather than the victim who succumbs to the troubling 'root of bitterness' (Hebrews 12:15).

Scriptures to reflect on
- 'If you do not forgive others, neither will your Father forgive your trespasses' (Matthew 6:15).
- 'Father, forgive them; for they do not know what they are doing' (Luke 23:34).
- 'Lord, do not hold this sin against them' (Acts 7:60).
- 'If it is possible, so far as it depends on you, live peaceably with all' (Romans 12:18).
- 'Bear with one another and, if anyone has a complaint against one another, forgive each other; just as the Lord has forgiven you, so you also must forgive' (Colossians 3:13).

19. Visit those in need

The other day I was talking with a member of another church. 'In the past eleven years', he said, 'my minister has never visited me once, not even when first my father, and then my mother, died. Ministers it seems have given up on visiting.'

Sadly, this is not the first time that I have heard this criticism. The impression I gain is that many of my colleagues see their task in managerial rather than pastoral terms. I was once present at a conference for ministers of larger churches where my admission that I love to visit people in their homes was greeted with disbelief, and I was made to feel as if I belonged in the ark.

Yes, there are limits to the amount of visiting pastors in larger churches can do. It certainly isn't possible to visit every member every year. In many cases it is a more efficient use of ministers' time to have people make appointments to see them in their church office. Yet, there is something special about a home visit. The dying and the bereaved, for instance, warrant home visits. And if for any reason I have failed to make it in time to the maternity ward, then I shall certainly want to see the couple with their first child at home. Newcomers too I shall always visit in their homes, for home is where people are most real; home is where one can above all get to know people for who they are.

Routine pastoral visiting I happily delegate. And yet there are times when I visit older members of the church who are housebound. The other day, for instance, I spent a full hour with one of our older members who had just moved into a home. Yes, I could have popped in just for 10 minutes, and yet it seemed to be important that on that occasion I gave her a significant period of my time, when I could listen to her and her concerns. Similarly, for me it is important that every housebound member and friend of the church is brought communion by a minister in the week running up to Christmas and Easter – some of those visits prove to be very special.

Most of my visits are not 'sacramental', in the sense that I only take communion to the housebound. And yet, hopefully every visit I make is 'sacramental' in the sense that it becomes 'a means of grace' to those I see. Every visit ends with prayer, and in many a home I read the Scriptures. This is surely all part and parcel of being a 'minister'.

How much visiting should a pastor do? The only yardstick I have come across is a principle enunciated by Kennon Callahan, an American Methodist who has written a number of ministerial textbooks: 'spend one hour in pastoral visitation each week for every minute you preach on a Sunday morning'.[1] Goodness, if we pastors were to adopt that principle, most of our sermons would probably be considerably shorter![2]

Communion visiting

The way in which we take communion to the shut-in will vary enormously. In my tradition the receiving of the elements is but part of the visit. Because I am not having to give communion to the housebound on a weekly basis, I can afford to take more time over my visit. Indeed, I normally spend around half an hour with the person I am visiting.

Also, I never make a communion visit on my own. At the very least I will take a lay visitor with me to symbolize the wider church. Best of all, I encourage several members of the church to be present. Sometimes they are neighbours; sometimes they are relatives – I leave the choice to the person we are visiting. In this way the visit becomes a special occasion.

On arriving, I do not immediately go into the communion service. We spend time sharing news. Clearly, it is important to listen to the concerns of the person being visited – but it can also be good for the person being visited to be made aware of the concerns of the church, if not of the world. These concerns will then inform the prayers we make at the end of communion.

After initial conversation, we begin with a prayer on which we ask God's blessing on our service, and seek his forgiveness for where we have failed him. We move then to the 'Word' – I read a passage of Scripture and then 'expound' the Scriptures for a few minutes. Often the passage chosen is the passage from which I preached the previous Sunday. From the 'Word' we then move to the 'sacrament'. I read the Words of Institution and then lead in a prayer of thanksgiving. After serving bread and wine, we then pray for the housebound person, and then for the church and the wider world. We finish our service by holding hands and saying together the words of the Grace. If we have not already had a cup of tea, we have it then. And then off I go to make my next visit.

Scriptures to reflect on
- 'I did not shrink from doing anything helpful, proclaiming the message to you and teaching you publicly and from house to house' (Acts 20:20).
- 'Do this in remembrance of me' (1 Corinthians 11:24).
- 'My little children, for whom I am again in the pain of childbirth until Christ is formed in you' (Galatians 4:19).
- 'So deeply do we care for you that we are determined to share with you not only the gospel of God but also our own selves' (1 Thessalonians 2:8).
- 'We dealt with each one of you like a father with his children' (1 Thessalonians 2:11).

20. Pray for healing for one another

Alas, I have never seen a medically verifiable miracle of healing. I have often prayed for people to be healed. Indeed, there have been occasions when I have followed the injunction of James 5:13–16 and taken some of my church leaders into people's homes and prayed for the sick, but in spite of our prayers we have not seen a real miracle of healing take place. I have seen people get better, but not permanently. I have seen people helped, but not physically healed as a direct result of our prayers.

And yet I have met many people who claim to have seen God work amazing miracles of healing. Some of these claims I respect; but, if the truth be told, many test my credulity: why, even this week I was told of a lady who had prayed for her dog, and the wart on its nose had vanished!

A further personal complication in this healing business is that for years I have suffered chronic back pain; and, although I have been prayed for on countless occasions, my back still gives me problems.

So does God heal today? I believe he does. But, my experience is that God acts through normal medical and surgical skills as much as through prayer; or rather, that he works through medical and surgical skills together with prayer. So, when James urged church elders to pray and rub olive oil on the sick, the oil was the first-century equivalent of deep heat treatment and sticking plaster, as we see for instance in the parable of the good Samaritan (Luke 10:34). In other words, for James, prayer went hand in hand with medical treatment – James did not view prayer as the last resort when all else failed. This does not mean that God limits himself to normal medical practices; there are times when the skill of doctors and nurses goes only so far, but God in his mercy goes further.

Yet, as we know all too well, God does not always heal our loved ones. Healing, like suffering, is a mystery. Sadly, there are some misguided Christians who believe the key to healing lies in our exercise of faith, and that if prayers are not answered, then it is because we have not prayed with sufficient faith. However, although clearly faith has an important role to play (indeed, James 5:15 boldly declares that 'prayer made in faith will heal the sick'), faith in itself heals nobody. Faith is but a channel for the healing power of God. Sometimes God allows our faith to become a channel for his healing, and sometimes he does not.

Why God heals some and not others, I don't know. And yet I dare to believe that God does always answer prayer. He may not answer it in the way in which we want, but answer he does. This was Paul's experience, for instead of removing his 'thorn in the flesh', God gave him strength to cope. What was true for Paul has been true for many others. Through his Spirit God has held people's lives firm, even when they had to go through the most appalling tragedies. God has kept their spirits serene and trusting, even when everything has seemed to go wrong. This surely is as much a 'miracle' as physical healing.[1]

A form of words for the commissioning of a prayer team
We have come to set aside a group of people who after having undergone appropriate training have formed a prayer ministry team, with a view to praying with others. In future, members of the team will be available to pray in the area under the cross (hung at one end of our church) immediately after the service. In a real sense they will be representatives of the Lord Jesus, offering his love and grace to all in need of God's touch upon their lives.

The good news is that Jesus continues to invite us to come to him. He says: 'Come to me, all of you who are tired from carrying heavy loads, and I will give you rest' (Matthew 11:28, Good News Bible). As one hesitant sufferer discovered, it was enough just to touch the edge of Jesus' cloak to experience healing. On that occasion Jesus said: 'Daughter, your faith has made you well; go in peace' (Luke 8:48). So let us come to Jesus believing that he is able to make all the difference. In the words of this year's church motto: 'Don't worry about anything, but in all your prayers ask God for what you need, always asking him with a thankful heart' (Philippians 4:6, Good News Bible). Yes, of course, we can come to him directly. But sometimes in our weakness we need others to pray for us. In this respect the words of James are pertinent: 'Confess your sins to one another, and pray for one another, so that you may be healed' (5:16). This is the context in which we now establish our new prayer ministry team.

Let us pray for our friends: 'Father God, we pray your blessing upon every member of our prayer ministry team. Help them to be open to others in listening, sensitive to unseen suffering, perceptive in understanding, so that in their praying they may be able to bring to you the true needs that are among us. May they become channels of your love and grace. In the name of Jesus, we pray. Amen.'

Scriptures to reflect on
- 'Moved with pity, Jesus stretched out his hand and touched him' (Mark 1:41).
- 'Daughter, your faith has made you well; go in peace' (Luke 8:48).
- 'Cure the sick . . . and say to them, "The kingdom of God has come near to you"' (Luke 10:9).
- 'Are any among you sick? They should call for the elders of the church and have them pray over them, anointing them with oil in the name of the Lord' (James 5:14).
- 'By his wounds you have been healed' (1 Peter 2:24).

21. Don't neglect the elderly

The world has adopted the youth culture, and in this respect the church is little different from the world. Older people tend not to be valued in the world, and for the most part they are not valued in the church.

Currently, we as a church are wanting to appoint a youth specialist. To this end, we have just inserted an advertisement in a major Christian monthly. I see with interest in this month's edition of that magazine that some fifty other churches are after a youth specialist, but not one is after a specialist for older people. Is that another reflection that older people do not count? Although it may be true that overall there are more older people than younger people attending church, there are still many who don't. According to one survey, in 1998 out of almost eight million people in England aged 65 and over, fewer than 1 million attended a church.

Yes, of course we need to be concerned for young people – but we need to be concerned for older people too. In the words of Rhena Taylor: 'As young people are not the church tomorrow, neither are older people the church of yesterday.' Unfortunately, many churches do not exercise a truly all-age ministry, with the result that activities for the under-eighteens tend to outnumber activities for the retired by at least two to one. Furthermore, the activities churches do have for older people fall into essentially two categories: they are either an expression of social concern for 'outsiders' (e.g. luncheon clubs for the elderly) or devotional meetings for 'insiders'. There is little with a distinctively evangelistic edge.

In my own church we have developed a clear strategy for winning older people for Christ. We have bridge-building activities, such as our annual 'Holiday at Home', which we run one week after the annual holiday club for children. The activities at both these events are very different, yet the aim is essentially one. Another bridge-building activity is our monthly lunch followed by a social activity of one kind or another (a quiz or a talk, a demonstration or an outing). Here friendships are forged with a good number of non-churchgoers. The next step is to invite people to a monthly Sunday afternoon 'event' (it is neither a 'meeting' nor a 'service'), which is fast-moving and hi-tech in presentation and lasts only 45 minutes. It is to all intents and purposes a 'seeker service' for those 'older in years, but young in heart', where the claims of Christ are always clearly spelt out. The great draw of this Sunday afternoon 'event' is that it is followed by 'the best tea in town'! Not surprisingly, it attracts large numbers, many of whom have no connection with our church. Our next project is to run a daytime Alpha specifically for older people.[1]

Develop a strategy for the 60-plus

1. *Encourage older people to socialize.* Just like young people, older people have social needs. These social needs become all the more important as friends and loved ones die. Older people can feel very lonely. Churches need to provide opportunities for social activity, where older people can genuinely enjoy themselves and find new friends.

2. *Encourage older people to grow as persons.* Emotionally, for instance, all of us have still got a lot of growing to do. The sad fact is that some older people are stunted people as a result of experiences that have embittered them. Here is a massive pastoral challenge to ensure that older people continue to be 'green and full of sap' (Psalm 92:14) in their later years.

3. *Encourage older people to continue to use their minds.* Just as life doesn't end at 60, neither too should lifelong learning! This may involve going to the local branch of the University of the Third Age

rather than involvement in the church. But so what? Ministers should be concerned for the good of people, rather than see them as fodder for the church machine. And at any rate, it ensures that older people do not get stuck in a church ghetto.

4. *Encourage people to grow spiritually.* With the beginning of the retirement years there is an opportunity to develop one's prayer life, to explore new and unfamiliar paths of spirituality and to go on retreat.

5. *Encourage older people to face their mortality.* Just as sex should regularly feature on any programme for young people, so too death and the world to come should feature regularly on any programme for older people. But it is not simply death and the world to come that should be on the agenda. Older people need to be helped to cope with the stages of role-reversal and of dependence, when they can no longer be the kinds of active people they were.

6. *Encourage older people to continue to serve the Lord.* This can do the church good, and it can do individuals good too. Indeed, Paul Tournier believed that every retired person needs a second career, with goals and a mission, that must be distinguished from leisure activity.

7. *Encourage older people to seek and use opportunities for evangelism.* Just as teenage years can be fruitful for the gospel, so too can retirement years. For just as teenage years can be turbulent, so too can retirement years, for retirement brings the onset of a series of life-changing events. These events can provide 'windows of opportunity' in which people can move from resistance or indifference to the gospel, on the one hand, to receptivity and openness on the other hand.

Scriptures to reflect on
- Caleb (85 years old): 'Give me this mountain' (Numbers 14:12, Authorized Version).
- 'In old age they [the righteous] still produce fruit; / they are always green and full of sap' (Psalm 92:14).
- 'Even when you turn grey I will carry you' (Isaiah 46:4).
- 'We do not lose heart. Even though our outer nature is wasting away, our inner nature is being renewed day by day' (2 Corinthians 4:16).
- 'Cast all your anxiety on him, because he cares for you' (1 Peter 5:7).

22. Help the terminally ill

Toward the end of last year I visited a good friend, who was dying of cancer. He had been suffering from cancer for a number of years, but now he was losing the battle. It was clear that death was only weeks away, and yet my friend did not want to acknowledge what was happening to him. 'I just don't know what's wrong with me,' he said. At that point I was faced with a choice: I could either pretend that I too didn't know, or I could pierce the bubble of unreality and say: 'Of course, you know what's wrong with you – you are seriously ill with cancer and your future is now very limited.'

I opted for the latter course. As a pastor I felt I just could not go along with the pretence. In this case, my friend was a member of my church, and so we could talk about his impending death, knowing that it was not the end, but rather the gateway to new life.

We talked about the Christian hope, and in doing so I believe that I was able to encourage and strengthen him in his faith. We talked too about arrangements for his funeral. As a result, when I next called, my friend was able to give me a list of hymns he had chosen for his eventual service of thanksgiving and also the Scripture reading he desired. I was glad he did, because this made it possible for his funeral some five weeks later to be so much more personal. Indeed, his choice of hymns and of Scripture reading were a witness to the many non-Christians present at the funeral – it was a case of 'he being dead, still speaks'.

Sadly, the experience I had with that friend is not the norm. All too often I do not have the opportunity to talk to the terminally ill about the difference that Jesus can make to our dying as well as to our living. Even among Christians there can still be a conspiracy of silence. And what is true of Christians is even truer among non-Christians. Time and again relatives and friends have told me that their loved one is dying, but does not know: and they, the relatives and friends, don't want them to know. Even the medical staff can join in this deceitful collusion.

As a minister I then find myself in dreadful difficulty: I am under instructions not to say anything, and yet by keeping quiet I am perhaps denying the dying person an opportunity to enter God's kingdom. What can I do? Pray! Yes, I find that relatives of the dying are quite happy for me to pray for their loved one. So, within the context of a prayer, I thank God that he is with us at all stages in life's journey and that there is nothing in life or in death that can ever separate us from his great love for us in Jesus. Hopefully, in that small way I help the dying to prepare to meet their Maker.[1]

Encourage people to prepare for death

'I've packed my bags and I'm ready to go,' said Pope John XXIII. It's a quotation I've often used at funeral services to underline the point that all of us need to prepare for death. For death and income tax are the two great certainties of life!

How do we prepare for death? When I quote Pope John I have in mind the need for each one of us to commit our lives into the safekeeping of Jesus and in turn to know the security that Jesus alone can give us, both in this life and the next. Like most ministers I begin a funeral service with the stirring words of Jesus 'I am the resurrection and the life. Those who believe in me, even though they die, will live' (John 11:25). What a difference it makes to know that death is not the end. There is no more important step to prepare for death than by responding to Jesus and his offer of forgiveness of sins and life beyond the grave.

But there are other ways in which we can prepare for death. We can prepare for death by living life to the full in the here and now. By living life to the full I do not mean the traditional way of 'living it up' with wine, women and song, but rather living a full life for God; being the person God would have us be; fulfilling the role that God would have us to play at home and at work, in the community and in the church. Scott Peck wrote with some perspicacity: 'I don't think people are afraid of death itself. What they are afraid of is the incompleteness of their life.'[2] Few of us, even if we live to a ripe old age, will die with a sense of total completeness. Sadly, there will always be things we have left undone. Yet, what a difference it will make if when we die we can know that we have been reasonably faithful in the stewardship of the life that God has given us.

Another way of preparing for death is to ask ourselves the kinds of questions suggested by Bill Kirkpatrick, an Anglican priest who specializes in working with the dying:[3]

1. Who would I like to be at my side, to embrace me as I'm dying?
2. Who do I think would really miss me?
3. What impression would I leave behind?
4. What single word would give meaning to my life?
5. What have I to put right before I die?
6. What relationships have I to put right before I die?
7. Who have I to say thanks to before I die?
8. From whom should I seek forgiveness?
9. To whom should I offer forgiveness?
10. What should I like to achieve before I die?
11. What kind of service would I like?
12. Whom would I specifically invite?
13. Whom would I not invite and why?

Some of these questions are not easy to answer. All the more reason for the pastor to help his people to face up to them, and so be better prepared for dying.

Another way of preparing for our death is by planning our own funeral arrangements. And by this I don't mean buying a funeral plan from the Co-op, although that may take a burden off our loved ones when it comes to deciding the type of coffin and the means by which the body should be disposed of, but rather planning how others will remember us on the day of our funeral.

Some years ago I decided to prepare for my own death by not only choosing the hymns and readings for my funeral, but writing out a complete order of service and including the music to which I would like my mourners to come in and go out. I gave detailed instructions for the committal of my body and for the wake to follow the service. I envy the minister who will have to take my funeral – I will really have simplified her (or his) job!

Bill Kirkpatrick also advocates what he terms the 'co-creating' of the funeral service. He tells the story of one man, who had been in the catering industry and who wished his friends to toast him with a glass of champagne. So, after the words of committal, the mourners were invited to surround the bier. Chilled champagne and glasses were wheeled in on a serving trolly, corks popped, glasses filled and passed around, and everyone drank a toast to the man's life as the coffin was lowered![4]

Yes, let's help our people to prepare for their dying!

Scriptures to reflect on
- 'You show me the path of life. / In your presence there is fullness of joy; / in your right hand are pleasures for evermore' (Psalm 16:11).
- 'Lord Jesus, receive my spirit' (Acts 7:59).
- 'Thanks be to God, who gives us the victory through our Lord Jesus Christ' (1 Corinthians 15:57).
- 'For to me, living is Christ and dying is gain' (Philippians 1:21).
- 'Do not be afraid; I am the first and the last, and the living one. I was dead, and see, I am alive for ever and ever' (Revelation 1:17–18).

23. Welcome funeral tributes

As a young minister I used to feel that tributes at a funeral were wrong. A Christian funeral was not a place for eulogies, but for preaching. I used to say that my prime task was to speak about the grace of God, and not to speak about the departed. And in this belief I was in good company. William Carey, for instance, said as he was dying: 'When I'm gone, don't talk of me, but of Carey's Saviour.'[1] So I never encouraged tributes from friends and relatives. Instead, I would say a few words about the loved one, before getting on with the real job of speaking about Jesus.

Over the years I have changed my mind. I now believe there is a place for tributes. True, by and large I do without tributes when the funeral service is at the crematorium, for then we are normally limited to 20 minutes. But when we have a church service, we now tend to have tributes. Indeed, my custom of beginning with the committal and then going on to the church for 'a service of thanksgiving' actually encourages tributes. Sometimes we have as many as three tributes before the sermon.

Why the change of mind? Perhaps because I now see a real distinction between a eulogy and a tribute. Although technically a 'eulogy' involves only 'a speaking well' of the person concerned, in fact a 'eulogy' tends to involve an exercise in praise so unreal that it contravenes the Trades Description Act. In a Christian funeral at least, there is no place for such a glorification of the departed, for 'all have sinned and fall short of the glory of God' (Romans 3:23). Along with our virtues we all have our vices. As a Christian minister I cannot afford to engage in unreal eulogizing, for it then calls my own integrity into question, which in turn means that there is good reason for the congregation to be sceptical about my affirmations of the gospel.

However, there is a place for tributes that are honest and deserved. If, as James affirms, 'every perfect gift is from above' (James 1:17), then it is only right for us to celebrate the lives of our loved ones and to thank God for them. So, whether or not there is a formal tribute in a service, I normally encourage the mourners to allow the memories of their loved ones to surface and then be grateful to God for those memories. There is a proper place for a tribute. Indeed, tributes at a funeral service can play a role akin to testimonies at a baptismal service – the person becomes more real.

Needless to say, there also needs to be an address. The task of the pastor is indeed to speak about the difference Jesus makes to living and to dying, and to minister the grace of God into the lives of those who mourn. At a funeral service we not only thank God for our loved one; we also praise God for the comfort of the gospel. But the two should go hand in hand, rather than be exclusive of the other.[2]

Dealing with a funeral of an 18-year-old

From a very young age Jonathan had been diagnosed as suffering from Duchenne, a wasting disease related to muscular dystrophy. Boys suffering from Duchenne do not normally live much beyond the mid to late teens. Jonathan, to the surprise of his parents, was blessed with a further four years of life.

As is our custom, we began the funeral with the committal at the crematorium. Only the family and some close friends were there. We sang 'Thine be the glory, risen conquering Son' and listened to a few Scripture verses before the committal itself. It was a very poignant moment as Jonathan's father and his two brothers placed three roses on the coffin prior to the curtains being pulled around.

The committal was followed by the church service. The family had decided that it did not want a 'thanksgiving service'. Rather, they asked for 'a celebration' of Jonathan's life. With 'celebration' in mind the church was decorated not just with colourful flowers, but with bright helium-filled balloons, some red in the shape of hearts and stars, others blue in the shape of porpoises (a reminder of an occasion when Jonathan had seen porpoises off the coast of Ireland). The music too was upbeat. Instead, of organ music, two of Jonathan's favourite CDs were played: as people came into church, we listened to 'The Lion King', and as people left, 'Affirmation' by Savage Garden was played. Along with the organ there was a worship band, including drums. We sang some of Jonathan's favourite songs, including 'Jubilate, everybody … Jubilate Deo' and 'We want to see Jesus lifted high, a banner that flies across this land'. It was very much a young person's service, even although most of the large congregation were not young people. In planning the service I had questioned with the parents whether we were right in majoring on celebration and was concerned that we should also have an opportunity to express our grief. However, I need not have been concerned. We had already expressed our grief at the crematorium and were now ready to move on.

We began with a modern classic, 'Be still, for the presence of the Lord is here'. The prayer that immediately followed focused on the line 'Be still … he comes to minister his grace'.

There were four Scripture passages. The first three were chosen by me: Psalm 23; John 14:1–2, 6; and 1 Corinthians 15:20, 42–43, 54–57. The family chose the final reading: 1 Corinthians 13:4–8a.

The three tributes were given by Jonathan's eldest brother, his GP and one of his teachers. This was an occasion for smiles and even laughter as we fondly recalled some of the past incidents of Jonathan's life. As the tributes were being given, photographs of Jonathan were beamed on to our large screen. It's amazing how useful video and PowerPoint projection can be at a funeral!

A Christian funeral service, however, cannot limit itself to reflecting on the past life of a loved one. There must also be an opportunity for declaring the gospel of Christ. Among other things, in my address I said:

> We do not want to minimize the grief that rightly surrounds the death
> of Jonathan. At any time to lose a loved one is hard – and harder still

to lose a son, let alone an 18-year-old son. But, in the words of the apostle Paul, we do not 'grieve as others do who have no hope' (1 Thessalonians 4:13). It is this hope that enables us to call today's service a 'celebration'. For although the tributes have celebrated Jonathan's past, we can also celebrate Jonathan's present and the future, for Jonathan was a believer – and where there is faith there is hope.

Sadly, for those who do not believe there is hope death is the end . . . The good news is that our loved ones need not be lost. As Jesus made clear, those who die believing are at home in their Father's house. Jonathan is in the Father's house, forever safe in the Father's love. This is what we celebrate (this is why we have balloons); this is why, instead of singing a funeral dirge, we sing songs of hope and of joy.

True, at the time of death there is sadness. There would be something wrong in our relationship if we did not shed tears when a loved one died. I find it significant that Jesus wept at the tomb of his friend Lazarus . . .

But there is 'crying' and 'crying', 'grieving' and 'grieving'. Paul says we do not have to grieve as 'others do who have no hope'. For the Christian, death is not the end. In the words of Jesus with which we began this service: 'I am the resurrection and the life. Those who believe in me, even though they die, will live' (John 11:25).

Jesus makes all the difference! He makes all the difference even on a day like today. Yes, even amid our sadness we have reason to celebrate.

After prayers thanking God for the comfort of the gospel and for the life of Jonathan, and then praying for the family, we concluded with 'Shine, Jesus, shine'.

Afterwards our church ladies served tea and refreshments to more than two hundred guests. One of the advantages of having the committal before the service is that the family has an opportunity to greet all those who have come to the service. It was a lovely way to end Jonathan's funeral.

Scriptures to reflect on
- 'Therefore, my beloved, be steadfast, immovable, always excelling in the work of the Lord, because you know that in the Lord your labour is not in vain' (1 Corinthians 15:58).

- 'I have fought the good fight, I have finished the race, I have kept the faith' (2 Timothy 4:7).
- 'Time would fail me to tell of Gideon, Barak, Samson, Jephthah, of David and Samuel and the prophets – who though faith conquered kingdoms, administered justice, obtained promises, shut the mouths of lions, quenched raging fire, escaped the edge of the sword, won strength out of weakness, became mighty in war, put foreign armies to flight' (Hebrews 11:32–34).
- 'Remember your leaders, those who spoke the word of God to you; consider the outcome of their way of life, and imitate their faith' (Hebrews 13:7).
- 'Every generous act of giving, with every perfect gift, is from above' (James 1:17).

24. Care for the bereaved

There is nothing harder than losing someone we love. If only it were not so! The truth, however, is that when we have loved deeply, we hurt deeply when the object of our love is no longer with us. In the first week or so, neither kind words from friends nor sleeping pills from the doctor seem to make much difference. We discover that grief is something that we have to work through for ourselves. And yet, what a difference it makes, when there are others there to help us through the months, if not years, that lie ahead.

Inevitably, the minister has a key role to play in caring, but not only the minister. For as the apostle Paul once said, it is the task of all the members of the 'body' to care for one another (1 Corinthians 12:25). But how can we care for those who have lost loved ones?

In the first place, by being there with them and acknowledging their pain. Sadly, sometimes people feel embarrassed to talk about the loss of others and so, as it were, walk by on the other side. But simply ignoring the pain of the other actually compounds the pain, and makes the bereaved feel all the more lonely. Far better to go up to the bereaved and together with them reminisce about the loved one they have lost. If in the process tears result, we should not be too concerned. For tears are part of the normal response to the loss of a significant person in our lives. Indeed, if we don't express our grief, then all kinds of psychological complications can arise. In the words of the Turkish proverb: 'He that conceals his grief finds no remedy for it.'

Unfortunately, some Christians encourage the bereaved to rejoice in the new life that their loved ones now enjoy, as if crying for the loss of a loved one is wrong and is a sign of a lack of faith. But this refusal to face up to the pain of death and to own loss is a nonsense. Life for our loved ones, now free from their earthly limitations, may be much better, but we may well be the poorer for our loss. If we are to be helpful to the bereaved, then we need to be realistic about their loss.

We also need to reassure the bereaved when they become concerned by their sense of disorganization, or of depression, that grieving does take time, and that it is natural not to get over the loss of a loved one quickly; and that it is natural too to think that we have come to terms with our loss, and then all of a sudden to find all the old feelings overwhelming us again. Indeed, it is generally reckoned that the grieving process can take anywhere between two to five years. During that time we need to be there for the bereaved, especially at the time of the anniversary of the death, or of a birthday or wedding anniversary.

There are no short cuts to caring for the bereaved. Caring takes time, for grieving takes time.[1]

Reassure those who worry about their loved ones when they die
Down through the centuries Christians have asked themselves what happens to their loved ones when they die. Some of their questions have been very specific. For example, 'How will they look? If heaven be paradise restored, then will they be like Adam and Eve, naked and without shame? Or will they be wearing the finest of clothes, as befits their new status as citizens of heaven? How old will they appear? If someone dies in their nineties, will they appear bent and stiff with age? And if someone dies at the age of ten, will they appear as a child?' By the end of the thirteenth century, theologians reached a consensus: as each person reaches the peak of perfection around the age of 30, they will be resurrected as they would have appeared at that time – even if they never lived to reach that age!

The truth is that there are many questions to which we do not know the answer. In the words of Isaiah, quoted by Paul:

What no eye has seen, nor ear heard,
  nor the human heart conceived . . .
God has prepared for those who love him.
(1 Corinthians 2:9)

Heaven is beyond our imagining. We limit God the moment we begin to try to depict the new world that is coming. And yet amid the many unknowns, there are things we can know – things that pastors therefore need to teach their people.

First, we can be certain that for Christians death is not the end, but the gateway into a new and fuller life. In the words of Paul: 'Christ has been raised from death as the guarantee that those who sleep in death will also be raised' (1 Corinthians 15:20, Good News Bible). Jesus has defeated the powers of sin and death – and we too may share in that victory. As Jesus himself said: 'because I live, you also will live' (John 14:19).

Secondly, the resurrection of the body is not the same as the 'resuscitation' of a body. When on the last day God raises us from the dead, he will exercise his own creativity and will give us a new body. Strangely, some have failed to take Paul seriously when he wrote: 'flesh and blood cannot inherit the kingdom of God' (1 Corinthians 15:50). Tertullian, for instance, used such sayings of Jesus as 'even the hairs of your head are all counted' (Luke 12:7) and 'there will be weeping and gnashing of teeth' (Matthew 13:50) to prove that both hair and teeth will be present in the resurrection! But 'we will all be changed' (1 Corinthians 15:51). Furthermore, this resurrection of the body will be a superior form of existence. The limitations of this present life, with all its indignities and weaknesses, will be left behind. The life to come will not be a pale imitation of this life, but rather we will be more alive than ever.

Thirdly, the resurrection will entail continuity. This thought is present in Paul's analogy of the seed (1 Corinthians 15:36–37): death is not the end; death simply means change. In one sense there is no relationship between our bodies as children and our bodies as young people, let alone our bodies as old people. And yet there is continuity expressed through personality. At death our bodies undergo far more radical change. The 'seed' of our earthly bodies dissolves. Yet the new life that God gives has a relationship with the old. In spite of all the changes, it is the same person. This means that in answer to the question 'Shall we recognize our loved ones?', the answer must be 'Yes'.

Fourthly, resurrection means community. Although we may be buried in our individual little boxes, in the life to come we will not be living in separate pigeon holes – we will be living life together. This sense of community is present in the teaching of Jesus, where the kingdom of God is repeatedly likened to a great banquet (Luke 13:29). It is also implied by Paul's teaching concerning the resurrection of the body. For the body is a way in which we communicate with others. It is because we have bodies that we are able to talk to one another, smile at one another, and stroke and kiss one another. If the future life were just a solitary existence, then maybe a 'soul' would have been sufficient, but in fact it is about life together – and so must involve the resurrection of the body. True, it will be a new way of living together. There will be no exclusive relationships such as we find in marriage (see Luke 20:27–38), but relationships there will be.

In this way pastors can reassure their people that there is no reason to worry about our loved ones.

Scriptures to reflect on

- 'I am the resurrection and the life. Those who believe in me, even though they die, will live' (John 11:25).
- 'Do not let your hearts be troubled. Believe in God, believe also in me. In my Father's house there are many dwelling-places' (John 14:1–2).
- 'Neither death nor life . . . nor anything else in all creation, will be able to separate us from the love of God in Christ Jesus our Lord' (Romans 8:38–39).
- 'Blessed be the God and Father of our Lord Jesus Christ! By his great mercy he has given us a new birth into a living hope through the resurrection of Jesus Christ from the dead' (1 Peter 1:3).
- 'He [God] will wipe every tear from their eyes. Death will be no more; mourning and crying and pain will be no more' (Revelation 21:4).

Part 4: Mission

25. Put faith into action

In the musical *My Fair Lady*, Eliza Doolittle exclaims: 'Words, words, words; I'm sick of words! I get words all day through, first from him, then from you! Is that all you blighters can do?' I believe that Jesus too is sick of words, words, words – he is sick of pious professions of faith that do not issue in practice.

Here is a challenge to many of us Baptist Christians. We stand in a tradition where words are important. It has been said that the first test of an evangelical church is the length of the sermon; and the second test is the presence of a meeting for Bible study and prayer. Much as I believe that listening to sermons and taking part in Bible study are vital to healthy Christian development, if our Christian faith revolves around such things alone, then there is something wrong about our faith. For at the heart of the Christian faith is the doctrine of the incarnation – the Word becoming flesh. Our words too need to be rooted in the business of living. Orthopraxis (right living) is as important as orthodoxy (right believing). Indeed, the latter without the former is a nonsense, for it is the former that tests the reality of the latter.

My mind goes to one of my former deacons, an extraordinarily eminent university professor who had been honoured with his own personal 'chair'; yet also an extraordinarily humble servant of the Lord Jesus who, without drawing any attention to himself, used to wash the sheets of an incontinent member of our women's meeting. If the truth be told, some felt his theology was a little suspect – he didn't dot the 'i's and cross the 't's in the way we thought was right; and yet the way he lived the faith put the more orthodox of us to shame.

Yes, actions count, and actions often convert. No doubt this is what the apostle Peter had in mind when, instead of telling his readers to be ready to take the initiative in sharing their faith, he said: 'Be ready at all times to answer anyone who asks you to explain the hope you have in you' (1 Peter 3:15).

A little while ago I read a book with a wonderful title, *The Provocative Church*. There Graham Tomlin, the author, writes: 'Unless there is something about church, or Christians, or Christian faith, that intrigues, provokes or entices, then all the evangelism in the world will fall on deaf ears. If churches cannot convey a sense of "reality" then all our "truth" will count for nothing.'[1]

Some years ago, I was doing my level best to win for Christ a high-flying businessmen-cum-academic, but getting absolutely nowhere. But then the breakthrough came, and it had nothing to do with me. My friend happened upon a biography of Mother Teresa. In the reading of it he became convinced of the truth of God's love. It is actions, not words, that count.[2]

Actions, not words

In the parable of the sheep and the goats (Matthew 25:31–46), those who are condemned are not those who have committed murder, engaged in rape, cheated their employers or exploited their work-force, but rather those who did nothing. Jesus condemned not positive wrongdoing, but utter failure to do good. By contrast, the righteous are welcomed into the kingdom, precisely because they did something – in particular, they did something for the unfortunate of this world.

The fact that we have been saved by grace should not stop us from seeking to serve our God. Paul, when writing to the Ephesians about the grace of God, went on to say that 'we are ... created in Christ Jesus for good works' (Ephesians 2:10)! Justification through faith, though a gift of God's sheer grace, lays upon us the responsibility to work out in practice our new status as children of God. The only kind of faith in which God is interested is faith that shows its reality by the deeds it produces: 'The only thing that counts is faith working through love' (Galatians 5:6).

Religiosity is not enough. Actions, not words, are called for. The question arises: How do we put our faith into action? Here is a challenge to us as individuals. At the final judgment our deeds will be the evidence of the kind of people we are. I find this an uncomfortable, if not fearful, thought.

But there is also a challenge to churches. How do we express our faith as a church? Clearly, there is no one way in which churches put their faith into action – so much depends upon the size of church and on the needs of the area.

We need to remember that Jesus did not simply give the Great Commission (Matthew 28:19–20); he also gave the Great Commandment (Matthew 22:39; see also Mark 12:31 and Luke 10:27–28), which arises from Leviticus 19:18, 'love your neighbour as yourself'. For Jesus, loving our neighbour is second in importance only to loving God with all our being. With this in mind we defined the mission of our church as 'going Christ's way and making disciples'. 'Going Christ's way' means that we seek to model our mission on the mission of Jesus. Inevitably, this means that our mission must be 'holistic', reflecting God's love and concern for every aspect of people's lives. Just as Jesus fed hungry mouths, washed dirty feet, and comforted the sad, so too must we. If our mission is to be patterned on the mission of Jesus, then our evangelism must go hand in hand with costly, compassionate service.

Scriptures to reflect on
- 'Not everyone who says to me, "Lord, Lord", will enter the kingdom of heaven, but only one who does the will of my Father in heaven' (Matthew 7:21).
- 'And who is my neighbour?' (Luke 10:29).
- 'Peace be with you. As the Father has sent me, so I send you' (John 20:21).
- 'What good is it, my brothers and sisters, if you say you have

faith but do not have works? ... faith without works is also dead' (James 2:14, 26).

- 'How does God's love abide in anyone who has the world's goods and sees a brother or sister in need and yet refuses help?' (1 John 3:17).

26. Make evangelism a necessity

Evangelism is not an option – it's a necessity. If a church doesn't engage in effective evangelism, then death beckons. In the words of Texan author William Easum:

> Congregations whose membership has plateaued or is declining have much in common with dinosaurs. Both have great heritages. Both require enormous amounts of food ... Both become endangered species ... Like the dinosaur they have a voracious appetite. Much of their time, energy, and money is spent foraging for food (for themselves), so that little time is left to feed the unchurched ... Either their pride or their nearsightedness keeps them from changing the ways they minister to people ... All around are unchurched, hurting people ... But many refuse to change their methods and structures to minister to people where they are in ways they can understand. Like the dinosaur, their necks are too stiff or their eyes too near-sighted. Clearly God doesn't care if these congregations survive; but God passionately cares if they meet the spiritual needs of those God sends their way.[1]

Sadly, there are many churches in our country who are living in the past and are in essence living only for themselves. These churches are on the verge of extinction; indeed, almost certainly thousands of them will close their doors within the next ten or twenty years, as indeed thousands of them have already done. So for their self-preservation, let alone for the sake of the salvation of others, churches need to turn outwards and begin to engage in effective evangelism. How can this be done? The apostle Paul surely supplies the answer: 'So that I might by any means save some' (1 Corinthians 9:22).

The evangelistic task begins with building bridges of friendship with people outside the church. We have found that one very effective form of bridge-building is holding quiz evenings twice a year. These evenings are always extremely popular with 'outsiders', with the result that normally 50% of those present are non-churchgoers. Furthermore, they are so simple to organize – all one has to do is hire a quiz master and provide food (a 'ploughmans') and sell drink.

Then there is 'Alpha'. We run three courses a year: two of an evening, and another of a lunchtime. We've kicked the videos into touch – we find a personal presentation much more effective. Surprising as it may seem, our experience is that just putting a large banner outside the church advertising the next course brings people in – there is something to be said for getting on to a nationwide bandwagon.

Evangelism too entails putting on special services. Like many churches we have experimented with 'seeker-services'; indeed, we aim to put on one a term. However, there is no doubt that the most successful services in attracting non-church people are baptismal services. So, instead of directing the sermon to the candidates, I always ensure that the sermon is directed to their friends and relatives.

And so I could go on. In today's climate effective evangelism is no easy task. But no evangelism today, no church tomorrow.[2]

Encourage people with passion

What we need most of all are not the right programmes, but the right people.

The story is told of a newly employed American salesman, who stunned his boss with his first written report, for it demonstrated that he was nearly illiterate. He wrote: 'I see this outfit who aint never bought ten cents worth of nothing from us and sole them some goods. I am now going to Checawgo.' Before his boss could fire him, a second report arrived and it read: 'I cam to Checawgo and sole them haff a million.' Hesitant to dismiss the man, yet afraid of what would happen if he didn't, the sales manager transferred the problem into the lap of the president of the company. The next day the staff were amazed to see the salesman's two reports on the notice board, with this memo from the company president: 'We ben spending two much time trying to spel instead of tryin to sel. I want everybody should read these letters from Good, who is doin a grate job, and you should do like he done!'

When it comes to evangelism, education (theological or otherwise) is not what counts – rather a passion to tell others about Jesus. In the words of a piece of Victorian verse:

> When I enter that beautiful city,
> And the saints all around me appear,
> I hope that someone will tell me
> It was YOU who invited me here.

There was a famous bishop of the Church of South India, Bishop Azariah, who after he had conducted a baptismal service, would make his baptismal candidates line up on the river bank, put their hand on their heads, and say after him: 'I am a baptized Christian; woe unto me if I preach not the gospel.' This same bishop once asked the members of a conference how many people they had brought to Christ since their baptism. One old woman got up with difficulty and said with sorrow, 'I have only brought five people to Christ since I was baptized.' Only! My church would be revolutionized if each member had 'only' brought five people to Christ! Not so long ago I was speaking to a church on the subject of evangelism – and afterwards a lady in her sixties remarked: 'I have never ever felt able to tell others about Jesus.' I felt very sad. She was a Christian of many years standing and in her own way had done much for the cause of Christ, but had never told anybody about Jesus.

There is an urgent need for every Christian to tell others about Jesus. Leaders need to encourage their people to take courage in their hands and, when the time is opportune, tell their friends what a difference Jesus has made to our lives. It doesn't have to be a lengthy statement. It could be as short as 'Because I've found my faith has been such a help to me, I wondered if you might care to come along to a special service in our church.' But whether it be short or long, something needs to be said, for so much is at stake.

All this presumes that people have non-Christian friends to speak to. Sadly, the older people grow in the faith, the more likely they are to move into a Christian ghetto. This process need not be inevitable and could, with imagination and hard work, be reversed. What would happen if pastors suggested that all home groups were suspended for the autumn session and that instead members enrol in evening classes at the local college with a view to making friends with some of the happy pagans around?

We need to be passionate about sharing our faith. Faith without passion is worthless. In the words of St John Chrysostom, the fourth-century Bishop of Constantinople: 'Nothing is more useless than a Christian who does not try to save others ... I cannot believe in the salvation of anyone who does not work for their neighbour's salvation.'

Scriptures to reflect on

- 'Follow me and I will make you fish for people' (Mark 1:17).
- 'Go ... to your friends [literally, "your own"; i.e. your own family, your own friends, your own circle of acquaintances], and tell them how much the Lord has done for you' (Mark 5:19).
- 'Woe betide me if I do not proclaim the gospel!' (1 Corinthians 9:16).
- 'We are ambassadors for Christ, since God is making his appeal through us; we entreat you on behalf of Christ, be reconciled to God' (2 Corinthians 5:20).
- 'Always be ready to make your defence to anyone who demands from you an account of the hope that is in you; yet do it with gentleness and reverence' (1 Peter 3:15–16).

27. Go for growth

In recent years the subject of church growth has had a bad press, so much so that the British Church Growth Association has had to fold up and in its place we now have Healthy Church UK. In some ways I welcome the shift of emphasis. For God does not call us to grow churches – he calls us to make disciples. Of course, where disciples are made, the church normally grows, but growth in that case is a by-product of obedience to the Great Commission rather than the goal itself.

Still, to be fair to the leaders of the old church-growth movement, they always made it clear that what counted was not transfer growth, but conversion growth. Indeed, they used to distinguish 'conversion' growth from 'biological' growth. 'Biological' growth in their terms is when children from Christian families came to faith in Christ, whereas conversion growth for them is what happens when people are won from outside the church.

A more valid criticism of the old church-growth movement was its apparent commitment to the homogenous principle. Peter Wagner, for instance, an influential proponent of church growth, argued that 'the membership of a healthy growing church is composed of basically one kind of people'.[1] Although it is true that 'birds of a feather flock together', homogeneity within the church is in fact not to be welcomed and is not a sign of spiritual health – for the glory of the church's calling is to be a diverse and inclusive people. On this particular count I believe we can rightly be critical of the old church-growth movement.

And yet, some of the criticisms that have been made of church growth have been wrong. It is, for instance, not helpful to deduce from the lonely figure of the crucified Christ that Christ was not interested in success. The cross was not the end of the story; it was the means of Jesus drawing 'all people' to himself (see John 12:32). The cross may be a warning against false triumphalism and a pointer to the costliness of true growth; it does not speak against the need of churches to grow.

The truth is that churches need to grow. In this respect I am challenged by Professor Robin Gill, who likened churches to the pelicans in St James's Park in central London – peculiar creatures, stranded in an environment not their own; awkward, out of place, angular, with a big mouth but little brain, demanding but inactive. He said:

> Churches in Britain need to make urgent choices about structure and direction. If they are to cease being pelicans, they need to be much clearer about how they might be effective in present-day Britain. They need to be more single-minded about growth ... about how they might reach the nine out of ten people in Britain who seldom or never go to church.[2]

Church growth is indeed desirable![3]

Pay the price for growth

There is a church-growth maxim that if a church is to experience growth, then there is a price to be paid both by pastor and people alike.[4] Church growth is costly.

As far as the pastor is concerned, the following 'sacrifices' need to be paid:

1. *Hard work.* Hard work entails not simply putting the hours in, but also making the most of the hours that are put in. Church

growth doesn't just happen; it involves 'blood, sweat and tears'.

2. *A willingness to share the leadership.* There is no church growth without delegation.
3. *A willingness to have members one can't pastor.* There is no church growth without pastoral care being shared. Unfortunately, some pastors don't find it easy to let go!
4. *A willingness to stick at it.* It takes time before pastors see a reward for their labours. As a rule of thumb, it takes five years before most pastors begin to see fruit for their ministry – and sometimes it takes even longer.
5. *A willingness to update training.* Ministers need to keep abreast of new ideas; they need to sharpen old skills and learn new skills. They need to be continually learning.
6. *A willingness to be a leader.* Some pastors prefer to respond to the church's needs, to react to their ideas, rather than to go out in front and say: 'This is the way; let's go there.' The fact is that being a leader risks exposure; it risks failure.

As far as the church is concerned, the following sacrifices need to be paid. There must be a willingness to

- *follow church growth leadership.* If a church is not willing to trust its pastor, then the church will get nowhere. Leaders need to be allowed to lead.
- *give.* There is a financial tag to church growth. If a church is to grow, then it must be willing to invest in people, in programmes and sometimes in property too.
- *give time.* Time can be more costly than money. It is not easy after a hard day's work to go and be involved in visitation, pastoral care, nurturing, training, let alone praying!
- *adjust fellowship patterns.* Structures will have to change as the church grows. People will have to be content not to know everybody.
- *open leadership circles.* If a church is to grow, then it must allow others to share, if not take over, the leadership. That is not always easy, when for years the leadership has been in the hands of the same small group of people.

- *change.* It is not easy moving out of familiar patterns of doing church. Yet growth will only happen where people are prepared to move out of their comfort zones. Alas, all too often the movement becomes a monument. In the words of management guru Peter Drucker: 'Left to themselves, institutions develop resistance to change. In a service institution particularly, yesterday's success becomes today's policy, virtues, conviction, if not holy writ, unless the institution imposes on itself the discipline of thinking through its mission.'[5]

Church growth is not easy. Pain and sacrifice are involved. In the words of Win Arn and Donald McGavran:

> Church growth takes work. Converts are not picked up as we stroll casually along the beach. Faith has to be white hot before it will ignite faith in others. The future will not automatically happen by merely wishing hard. Growth requires decision – now! Growth imposes risks – now! Growth requires action – now! Growth demands allocation of resources – now! Growth requires work – now! Then God gives the increase.[6]

Scriptures to reflect on
- 'I tell you, you are Peter, and on this rock I will build my church . . . ' (Matthew 16:18).
- 'Other seed fell into good soil and brought forth grain, growing up and increasing and yielding thirty and sixty and a hundredfold' (Mark 4:8).
- 'So those who welcomed his message were baptized, and that day about three thousand persons were added' (Acts 2:41).
- 'The word of God [after the appointment of the seven 'deacons'] continued to spread; the number of the disciples increased greatly in Jerusalem' (Acts 6:7).
- 'I planted, Apollos watered, but God gave the growth' (1 Corinthians 3:6).

28. Create a welcoming and accessible building

For many people it takes real guts to enter a Christian church – just like it would take real guts on my part to enter a betting shop. Just as the latter is an alien place for me, so too the former for others. So, how do we help people to step over the threshold of our churches? By developing our facilities in such a way that our churches become warm, inviting places.

Some three or four years ago we radically redeveloped our dark somewhat forbidding Edwardian building and now have a wonderful suite of premises that are a delight to visit. Sadly, they didn't please one former member, who left the church in protest over our decision to redevelop: 'This isn't a church,' she said, on entering our carpeted Friendship Centre. 'This is more like a hotel!' What, however, she took for criticism, we took as a compliment, because we now see ourselves as being in the hospitality business. We want to be a place where people are made to feel welcome. We have sought to make every part of our building accessible – and by this I don't mean that it is disability-friendly (although it is), but that it is visitor-friendly.

We deliberately do not call the space where we worship 'the sanctuary' – for such a term creates unnecessary barriers. Instead, we have deliberately adopted a neutral term for the space in which we can seat up to 450 people. We call it 'the meeting place'. Yes, on a Sunday it is the place where we meet with God, but it is also the place where we meet with one another. In turn it is also the place the community love to use for their purposes – for concerts and exhibitions, lectures and presentations, book evenings and university exams. However, although the term may be neutral, the space itself is not totally neutral – along with a large wooden cross, there are two massive 'jewelled' tapestries made by the firm that created the enthronement robes for the former Archbishop of Canterbury, which proclaim the words of Jesus 'I am the resurrection and the life'.

In addition to hiring out our meeting place, as also our halls and seminar rooms, we run a small café, four days a week. As a result, on average in any given week over a thousand non-church people go through our premises – and often many more. And of course what is happening is that over the course of the year thousands upon thousands of people in our community are stepping over the threshold of our church. They may not actually be coming to 'church', and yet they are becoming familiar with our church buildings. Church in this sense is no longer an alien place. Needless to say, it took a good deal of sacrificial giving to make all this possible. But more important, it took a change of mindset on the part of church members. This new mindset involves the recognition that first and foremost we don't exist for ourselves – we exist for others.[1]

Town-centre churches are different

As its name implies, Central Baptist Church, Chelmsford, is a town-centre church. Nobody lives around us; rather, we are surrounded by offices, the central library and a university campus. The challenge for us has been to develop a role specific to our situation. Thus, in addition to all the normal activities of a large church, four days a week we run a café. No doubt because it is the cheapest place in town, it is a busy café and our volunteers are often run off their feet. People come in for the food. They also come in to use our computers – we have three of them, all with a fast broadband connection to the Internet. Twice a week we run clubs for people with mental health problems referred to us by social services; every other Saturday we run a child contact centre for broken families referred to us by the courts.

In addition, we have started a community resource centre to help under-privileged people tap into mainstream services – in our context these under-privileged people are mainly black Africans, who have come to England and who take menial jobs, because they don't know how to get recognition for the qualifications they already have. (Lest there be misunderstanding, those who run the resource centre are not whites, but rather professional black Africans who have 'made it' in British society.) The important point to understand is that we can run a café, our mental health clubs, the child contact centre, the community resource centre, precisely because we are a town-centre church, and not a neighbourhood church on some local estate.

But there is another way in which we have developed our service to the community. As a result, of having spent just under £2 million on revamping our Edwardian building into premises fit for the twenty-first century, we have found that many groups in the community wish to use our premises. If, for instance, Jamie Oliver wants to launch his latest book in Chelmsford, then it is to our church he comes. If the local university wants to find space for an introductory course for three hundred nurses, then it is to our church they come. If the Chief Executive of Essex County Council wishes to address his staff, then it is to our church that he and his staff come.

As a result of such bookings, we have a minimum of a thousand non-church people come through our premises every week. From a gospel perspective, the encouraging feature is that for many of these non-church people our church is a revelation, because it is different. This difference lies not just in the comfortable surroundings, but in the distinctive 'feel' to the place. In part this arises from the various symbols around pointing to Jesus and his love; but above all it arises from the gracious welcome given by the church-centre staff and volunteers.

Another feature of being a town-centre church is that people with no church connection will sign up for one of our Alpha courses. Some of these people see our Alpha publicity as a result of coming to a secular course or event being held at the church. Others on their way to the shops see our Alpha banner and decide to give us a try. While yet others find us on the Web. And they come to us because we are accessible, because we are a town-centre church.

What is true about us will, in different and yet related ways, be true of other town-centre churches. We are different from most other churches. We are not neighbourhood churches. This difference provides us with a challenge, a challenge to do church differently. It's not easy, but it is rewarding.[2]

Scriptures to reflect on

- 'The Son of Man came eating and drinking, and they say, "Look, a glutton and a drunkard, a friend of tax-collectors and sinners!"' (Matthew 11:19).
- 'Invite everyone you find' (Matthew 22:9).
- 'Put out into the deep water and let down your nets for a catch' (Luke 5:4).
- 'I, when I am lifted up from the earth, will draw all people to myself' (John 12:32).
- 'Welcome one another . . . as Christ has welcomed you' (Romans 15:7).

29. Engage in process evangelism

When I was a child the classic way in which many people became Christians was by attending an evangelistic event and responding to an appeal to come forward at the end of the sermon. Faith for them involved very much a crisis in their lives.

I remember as a 10-year-old attending the Billy Graham Crusade at Harringey Arena in 1954, and watching hundreds, if not thousands, of people streaming forward to the front in response to the appeal. In the 1950s, 1960s and 1970s that was the kind of evangelism that worked. However, it is generally reckoned that the last major successful evangelistic event held in Britain was the Billy Graham Mission England crusade held in 1984. After that, things changed. People no longer responded to Billy Graham (or indeed to any other evangelist) in the way they once did.

The fact is that we as a country have changed. Whereas at one stage there were many lapsed Christians and many people on the fringes of the church, people who knew the basics of the faith and subscribed to them, today things are very different. Today there is widespread ignorance about the Christian faith. As a result, evangelists no longer reap a harvest in one go. Instead, they have to be in the sowing as well as in the reaping business.

Evangelism has changed. Alpha courses, Y courses, Just-looking courses, are the name of the game. People need to be given time to become Christians. The Alpha course, for instance, is ten weeks in length, and even then many find it too short. Indeed, it is not unusual for people to want to repeat an Alpha course, and even then they need more time before finally committing their lives to Christ. Evangelism is no longer an event; it is a process.

In many ways the present developments are healthy. With people further and further away from the Christian faith, it is inevitable that the journey to faith takes longer. People need time to reflect on the Christian gospel and its demands before they commit themselves to Christ. Becoming a Christian is a massive step. It is a stepping from spiritual darkness to light. It is an act of lifelong commitment. It does radically affect the way we live our lives. It is only right and proper that people take their time. If the ordinary physical birth process takes nine months, then we should not be surprised if the spiritual birth process takes a number of months too.

So although we still preach gospel sermons (we have a monthly welcome service in addition to baptismal services and other specials) the key work of evangelism in our church is done in our Alpha courses. And the encouraging thing is that so many people want to come along to Alpha. Indeed, our experience is that just putting up a large banner outside the church advertising the next course brings people in off the streets. Such evangelism is demanding in terms of time, but it is also deeply rewarding.[1]

Seven steps to making disciples

The following steps depict the process of Christian discipleship. Although the alliteration may seem corny, it does help to make the seven steps easier to remember.

1. *Contact*:
   - through building personal bridges of friendship
   - through involvement in church organizations
2. *Communication*:
   - through personal (verbalized) witness
   - through regular 'seeker-friendly' services

3. *Clarification*:
   - through one-to-one conversations
   - through participation in an Alpha course

   Conversion:
   (This is not a step we as a church can take!)
4. *Incorporation*:
   - through baptism (confession of the faith)
   - through church membership (covenant community)
5. *Consolidation*:
   - through nurture in a small group (confirmation)
   - through presenting the challenge of Christian giving
6. *Commissioning*:
   - through training in faith-sharing
   - through encouraging service in and beyond the church
7. *Canonization* (an ongoing process):
   - through worship and fellowship
   - through witness and service

Scriptures to reflect on

- Andrew 'found his brother and . . . brought Simon to Jesus' (John 1:41–42).
- Peter quotes Joel: 'Everyone who calls on the name of the Lord shall be saved' (Acts 2:21).
- Philip, 'starting with this Scripture [Isaiah 53] . . . proclaimed to him the good news about Jesus' (Acts 8:35).
- Barnabas 'went to Tarsus to look for Saul . . . and . . . brought him to Antioch' (Acts 11:25–26).
- Jesus said to his disciples: 'You are the light of the world' (Matthew 5:14).

30. Share good news at Christmas

For children Christmas is good news. For Christmas means parties – parties at school and parties at church, parties with friends and parties with the family; parties where there is lots to eat and games to play. Christmas also means presents – presents in a stocking and presents around a tree; presents from Father Christmas and presents from parents. And, of course, Christmas means pantomimes and nativity plays, trips to the theatre and to the cinema; even perhaps trips to the ballet and the concert hall.

Christmas too is good news for adults. For we too enjoy parties, presents and pantomimes. We love the special foods that go with Christmas; the lighting of candles and the listening to carols; and above all the being together with family and friends.

But Christmas is not good news for everybody. Christmas for many is a time of sadness and of pain. Christmas is not good news for workers, when redundancy looms; nor is it good news for families where coming together exacerbates all the old tensions. Christmas is not good news either for those who have gone through the pain of marriage breakdown, where mothers and fathers are without their children. And Christmas is not good news for those who have lost loved ones in the year that has gone by. Yes, Christmas can be bad news; it can be the time when the pain of living intensifies. The very fact that Christmas is meant to be a time of happiness only makes our unhappiness all the worse: it exposes the wound and rubs in the salt. But the good news is that precisely for those for whom Christmas is bad news, it is in fact good news. For Jesus has come into our loneliness and pain: 'The Word became flesh' (John 1:14); Jesus shared our flesh and blood (Hebrews 2:14). Jesus has entered our world and has shared our human condition. He knows what it is like to be depressed and troubled in heart, to be misunderstood by family and friends. He knows what it is to experience pain: physical pain, emotional pain, mental pain – even spiritual pain. He knows and in knowing he understands. And because he knows and understands he can offer help and strength to those for whom life is dark and bleak.

It is against this background that a first-century Jewish Christian preacher wrote: 'Let us therefore approach the throne of grace with boldness, so that we may receive mercy and find grace to help in time of need' (Hebrews 4:16). God is not unapproachable; he does not live in some ivory tower remote from human experience. For Jesus is there at his right hand, Jesus who can feel for us and with us.

Here is good news for the lonely and the weak, for those for whom life is dark and bleak. Life does not have to be lived in our own strength. For the Jesus who came is the Jesus who is ready and waiting to give help to us all. So in the words of an American paraphrase of our text: 'Let's not let it slip through our fingers ... Let's walk right up to him and get what he is so ready to give. Take the mercy, accept the help' (The Message).[1]

Make the most of carol services
Research shows that even though less than 7% of the British population attend church on a regular basis, the majority of non-churchgoers would be tempted to go to a carol service if invited by a friend. According to David Clark, director of the advertising agency CMC:

> There is a comfort zone about a carol service that is unique ... They are a natural way in for people who wouldn't normally see themselves as churchgoers. Attending carol services is not perceived as a

committedly religious act, merely part of what makes Christmas, Christmas. The church needs to take advantage of its own inheritance.[2]

The lesson is clear. Churches need to make the most of their carol services. Carol services should not be regarded only as acts of worship, but rather as opportunities for outreach. Church members need to be informed of the receptivity of non-churchgoers to invitations to carol services and in the light of that fact should be encouraged to invite their friends and neighbours. If every church member were to invite five friends, and of these five friends three were to accept the invitation, then the majority of people attending the church's carol services would not be Christians. The carol service then becomes a wonderful opportunity for sharing the good news of Jesus.

Needless to say, churches need to package their carol services in such a way that they are both attractive and accessible to non-churchgoers. 'Carols by Candlelight' appeals to the sentimentality of many, and all the more so if the service is advertised as followed by mulled wine and mince pies! But if church members take their responsibility seriously of inviting friends and neighbours to the carol service, then one service is not enough. Two, if not more, are needed.

Over the years our custom has been to hold two services of Carols by Candlelight. On the Sunday before Christmas we have two evening services: the first at five o'clock for young families, and the second at seven o'clock.

The five o'clock service is geared to children under 11 and is like a typical family service, except there is no crèche for the babies – the babies are present too. Not only are our 'own' children present, but many others too. Children from the midweek 'babies and toddlers' group come – so too do many from our summer holiday club. Preceded by the annual children's Christmas party, the service is only 45 minutes long. Along with traditional carols and a couple of traditional readings, there are puppets and drama. And, of course, the children do their own thing, as they trot around the church singing 'Little donkey', or whatever. There is always a brief evangelistic spot – in which we seek to spell out the meaning of Christmas. It's one of the most exhausting services we run, but also one of the most worthwhile!

Then, an hour or so later, comes the more sophisticated seven o'clock service. Along with the traditional carols (and it is the traditional carols that outsiders expect) and traditional readings, there is drama of one kind or another, and always a 5- or 10-minute evangelistic address. Along with the challenge to people to open their hearts to the Christ-child then and there, I emphasize the need to open their minds to the possibility that God may well have come in Christ and therefore to come along to the new Alpha course we shall run after Christmas. As people leave church we seek to ensure that they all receive an invitation to the next Alpha introductory supper.

The key to the success of these carol services lies with the church gaining the vision of using the carol services as a key evangelistic tool. People need to be encouraged to think through who they might invite – to engage in what Robert Schuller called 'possibility thinking', which 'makes miracles happen'.[3] Without such thinking, nothing happens.

Scriptures to reflect on

- 'She [Mary] will bear a son, and you are to name him Jesus, for he will save his people from their sins' (Matthew 1:21).
- 'I am bringing you good news of great joy for all the people: to you is born this day in the city of David a Saviour, who is the Messiah, the Lord' (Luke 2:10–11).
- 'And the Word became flesh and lived among us, and we have seen his glory, the glory as of a father's only son, full of grace and truth' (John 1:14).
- 'When the fullness of time had come, God sent his Son' (Galatians 4:4).
- 'For the grace of God has appeared, bringing salvation to all' (Titus 2:11).

31. Engage with tough questions

Matthew tells us wise men came, asking (Matthew 2:1–2). Yes, it is precisely the wise who are not afraid to ask questions. It is only the stupid whose minds are so made up that they are not prepared to question the evidence for themselves. The wise men who searched for Jesus were skilled in philosophy, medicine and natural science – they were the intellectuals of their day. They came because their curiosity had been aroused by a special star

Today, if we would be wise, we too need to ask questions. But in the first instance we need to ask not 'Where is the baby born to be the king of the Jews?', but 'Who is this baby born to be the king of the Jews?' To answer that question we do not need to search the heavens as did those wise men; we need to 'search' (Authorized Version) or 'examine' the Scriptures (Acts 17:11). We need to examine the evidence to find out who this Jesus is. Yes, if we would be wise, we need to read the Gospels – to read not simply their account of the birth of Jesus, but also their account of the life, death and resurrection of Jesus. Wise men will not be satisfied with impressions gained as a child; rather, they will come to the gospel story with adult minds and ask adult questions. I guarantee that wise men with open minds will discover that there is no other way to account for

Jesus than finding him to be the Son of God and the Saviour of the world.

Sadly, too many have made up their minds without examining the evidence. In this respect the New Testament translator J. B. Phillips once wrote:

> Over the years I have had hundreds of conversations with people, many of them of higher intellectual calibre than my own, who quite obviously had no idea of what Christianity is really about. I was in no case trying to catch them out; I was simply and gently trying to find out what they knew about the New Testament. My conclusion was that they knew virtually nothing. This I find pathetic and somewhat horrifying. It means that the most important Event in human history is politely and quietly by-passed. For it is not as though the evidence had been examined and found unconvincing; it had simply never been examined.[1]

But it is not sufficient just to read the Gospels. Librarians like to quote Voltaire: 'read to enjoy'. But in terms of the gospel, Kafka was on firmer ground when he wrote: 'read to ask questions'.

'Wise men came asking.' We too need to be wise and to ask questions. Peter Abelard, the French philosopher and theologian, was right when he said: 'the first key to wisdom is assiduous and frequent questioning. For by doubting we come in inquiry and by inquiry we arrive at truth'. It is only by asking that we discover the truth as it is in Jesus.[2]

Engage in apologetics

God has given us minds, so we should encourage people to use them in their search for truth. As Christians we have nothing to fear from the use of the mind. Jesus described himself as 'the truth' (John 14:6) in the sense that he is the true and living way to God.

A favourite hymn for many people is 'Jerusalem', which asks: 'And did those feet in ancient time walk upon England's mountains green?' The answer, of course, is 'No, they did not.' For William Blake's stirring hymn was based on a legend that told of Joseph of Arimathea taking Jesus as a young man on a boat trip to England. Unfortunately, many people seem to assume that the life of Jesus as we find it in the Gospels is based on legends too. Such people need to be encouraged to read the Gospels to discover that they deal in truth. This was the discovery of E. V. Rieu, the first editor of the Penguin Classics series. When he set out to produce a new translation of the Gospels, he was an unbeliever. But, as he stated in his preface to the Penguin edition of *The Four Gospels*, his long task had 'changed' him. Now he was convinced that the Gospels 'bore the seal of the Son of Man and of God'.[3]

The oldest book I possess is dated 1749. Entitled: *Observations on the History and Evidences of the Resurrection of Jesus Christ*, it was written by a man called Gilbert West. When Gilbert West began his book, he was not a Christian – indeed, he set out to disprove the Christian faith. But the task changed him. Significantly, the title page has a quotation from the Apocrypha: 'Blame not before thou hast examined the Truth; understand first, and then rebuke.'

Non-Christians (and Christians too) need to be encouraged to think through the issues. This means that preachers need to engage in apologetics. When it comes, for instance, to the story of the virgin birth, for instance, preachers need to deal with the alleged parallels in Greek legends, which depict the gods ravishing attractive young females, and show that by contrast in the Gospel birth stories there is nothing sexual about God's creative activity.

Sometimes, of course, there are no easy answers to the questions people raise, but this is no reason not to seek to deal with them. With regard to the virgin birth, preachers need to be seen to wrestle with the alleged parallel in 'parthenogenesis', whereby certain species such as bees, frogs and worms are able to develop without fertilization. The fact is that if Jesus had been conceived by parthenogenesis, then he would have had to be a girl, because women can only pass on X chromosomes – for in normal reproductive intercourse girls are conceived when the male sperm adds a second X to the ovum's X chromosome; boys are conceived when the sperm adds a Y chromosome.

The fact is that there are no easy answers. However, once we believe in the God of creation and resurrection, difficulties in believing in the virgin birth disappear. True, such an argument could be seen to encourage general credulity. Yet, once all other options have been examined and no adequate basis found for abandoning the essential tradition of a virginal conception, then faith in the living God must step in. As John Taylor, a former Bishop of St Albans, once wrote: 'I find it easier to accept that when God chose to reveal himself in a human life, he did it as a one-off exercise rather than go through what the bureaucrats call "the usual channels". A Saviour of the world, without a touch of the miraculous at the beginning, the middle and the end of his life, I would find totally perplexing'![4]

Yes, it is important to encourage people to raise questions. They need to discover that the Christian faith is true, and precisely because it is true it matters.

Scriptures to reflect on
- 'Wise men ... came ... asking' (Matthew 2:1–2).
- 'I too decided, after investigating everything carefully ... to write an orderly account ... that you may know the truth' (Luke 1:3–4).
- 'The shepherds said to one another, "Let us go now to Bethlehem and see this thing that has taken place ..." ' (Luke 2:15).
- 'You will know the truth, and the truth will make you free' (John 8:31).
- 'Truth is in Jesus' (Ephesians 4:21).

32. Welcome newcomers and encourage hospitality

Baptists are generally friendly people. Hence the hubbub before the service – we like to greet one another. I know that some older friends long for the day when there was 'a bit of reverence' – when people bowed their heads and prepared themselves to worship God. Yet I prefer a church in the moments leading up to worship to resemble a bar in a busy pub on a Friday night. For God wants us to be friends, friends with him, friends with one another.

Unfortunately, churches can be exclusive in their friendships. People can be so busy greeting one another that they fail to notice newcomers. I remember an experience Caroline and I had. After a tough first year as Baptist Missionary Society missionaries in Congo, I was invited to give some lectures at an Anglican college just outside Nairobi. Our hosts offered to look after our two young children so that we could attend an English-speaking church in Nairobi. We were so excited, and all the more so when we entered and sensed the vibrancy of this large church. But nobody spoke to us – neither before nor after the service. We sat there, longing for somebody to come up to us, but nobody did. They were all too busy chatting to one another. They failed to notice this lonely young couple – and as a result our loneliness was intensified. Perhaps we should have made an effort to speak to others – but we felt so low spiritually, that we hadn't the energy. From that time on, I have always resolved to ensure that nobody is able to visit a church of which I am the minister without getting a welcome.

But a friendly welcome is not enough. I was once away from home for two weeks, and on the two Sundays I went to two different churches. First and foremost, of course, I went to worship God. But I was also half-hoping that after the service somebody might invite me back home for a drink, or even better for a meal. On both occasions I was disappointed. The people were very friendly, but not hospitable. Fortunately, I was not looking for a church in which to settle – had I been, I would not have settled there.

Hospitality is what a church is called to offer. According to the New Testament, hospitality is not an optional extra for those so inclined, but a duty for all. I think of one couple who before they went to church ensured that they had more than enough food for their Sunday lunch, so that they would be free to invite any stranger back home with them. That's what friendship is really about. The superficiality of after-church chat is nothing compared with the real thing. Hospitality beats friendliness every time.[1]

Hospitality involves opening our homes

The difference between hospitality and friendliness is well illustrated in some words I read the other day: 'Friendliness says, "Hi, how are you?" Hospitality says, "Come into my life!" Hospitality says, "Let's do something together – come over to my house, attend this event with me, join me for a cup of coffee."'

As Christians we are called to be hospitable people. We have a saying 'An Englishman's home is his castle.' But a Christian's home has no drawbridge – the door is open to all, and in particular to our brothers and sisters in the faith. Yes, if we truly love one another, we shall want to open up our homes to one another.

Hospitality is not a gift to be exercised by the few. All of us are called to have open homes as well as open hearts. Indeed, in Jesus' parable of the sheep and the goats, those who did not show hospitality are condemned: 'I was a stranger and you did not welcome me' (Matthew 25:43).

Furthermore, in the New Testament hospitality always had

strangers in view. Although, there is a place for having friends round, we are called to invite people who have yet to become our friends. This can be demanding. As I write, yesterday we had eight people back for Sunday lunch, only one of whom had ever been to our home before. By the end of the afternoon we were exhausted – but we felt pleased, because in that time we had had an opportunity not only to get to know some new friends, but also to be able to introduce them to one another.

There are many people who would appreciate hospitality. We need to give a special welcome to newcomers to the church. But we also mustn't forget the needs of those who live on their own, not just young singles, but also older people, and not least those who have lost their life partner. All too often, hospitality is directed in the first place to couples. And, of course, we should not forget non-Christian neighbours and work colleagues. If we are to build bridges of friendship into the non-Christian community in which we live, then we must open up our homes to them. As a rule of thumb we can't expect people to come to church until we have first had them in our home. So how about a summer barbecue or a Christmas drinks party for the neighbours?

The exercise of hospitality does not have to involve a meal. A coffee after church is often equally welcome. For hospitality is different from entertaining. When we entertain, we use the best china and generally pull out the red carpet; when we give hospitality, we allow people to accept us as we are.

Hospitality is something that needs to be built into the calendar. With all the pressures of modern life, it is often just not possible to have people home every week. There is therefore a lot to be said for encouraging people to consider setting aside one Sunday a month for opening their homes to others.

Thank God, hospitality is more than a duty; it is also a means of blessing. The writer to the Hebrews reminds us that some who did welcome strangers into their homes 'entertained angels without knowing it' (Hebrews 13:2). The original reference is to Abraham and Sarah, who entertained three men who turned out to be of supernatural origin (see Genesis 18:1–5). Their blessing was the promise of a child the following year. Although the exercise of hospitality is no sure-fire remedy for infertility, the basic point remains true: when we open our homes, we are the richer for that experience – and so too are those who come into our homes.

Scriptures to reflect on
- 'A woman named Martha welcomed him [Jesus] into her home' (Luke 10:38).
- 'Day by day ... they broke bread at home' (Acts 2:46).
- 'Extend hospitality to strangers' (Romans 12:13).
- 'Do not neglect to show hospitality to strangers' (Hebrews 13:2).
- 'Be hospitable to one another without complaining' (1 Peter 4:9).

33. Present the challenge of overseas mission

The editor has given me yet another 'toughie'. As one who in his younger years spent two periods of his life engaged in overseas mission (first as a Time for God volunteer in southern Germany, and then later as a Baptist Missionary Society missionary in Congo/Zaire), I am fully committed to the desirability of young people serving God overseas. However, in the over eleven years in my present church we have not had one young person go out with the BMS for more than a one-month period.

Having said that, we have had a couple take early retirement and serve as volunteers with the BMS in Cyprus, working for a Christian satellite company based in Cyprus, beaming programmes to North Africa and the Middle East. We have a gifted middle-aged Ugandan member on a three-year contract in Nigeria, seconded by the BBC World Service to help tackle the Aids problem there by running a radio soap with information about Aids. Although not a missionary in a technical sense, he is certainly there as a Christian. This summer one of our younger members leaves for a six-month stint with FEBA in Uganda, where she will be working for a Christian radio station; while another of our younger members will be going to Greece for a month under the auspices of Operation Mobilization to share her faith with athletes and others. And at this very moment a group of around twenty of our young people are saving hard to go on a mission trip to Ghana, where they will help to construct a school for a large village with which some of our African members have links.

So in one sense we are facing up to the challenge of overseas mission. And yet it is with difficulty. It would no doubt be easier if as a church we were to have regular exposure to 'real live' missionaries, but the supply from our BMS seems to be limited with the result that, apart from our own volunteer couple, we have only had two such visits in eleven years. Instead, we have been sent 'home' representatives of one kind or another. We have worked hard to develop relationships with BMS Link missionaries assigned to us, but for the most part this has been abortive – for up until recently those with whom we have been linked have returned to the UK disillusioned.

Our experience too of BMS Action Teams has been mixed. We have just had a super group from Brazil, but a previous group was an utter disaster. But we are not giving up. Our latest initiative is, with the help of the BMS, to invite a young Brazilian to come to Britain to serve with us as an 'evangelistic intern'. His brief, 'to inspire young people to grow in their faith and to reach out to their friends with the good news of Jesus'; hopefully, he will also whet the appetite of some for overseas mission themselves.

To conclude: I'm not sure that we have cracked the nut of presenting the challenge of overseas mission to our people, but at least we are trying. I look forward to learning from other churches as to how they have enabled their people to face up to this challenge.[1]

Jesus is the only way

For centuries people believed that the sun went around the earth. But then in the sixteenth century Copernicus made the amazing discovery that it was the earth that went around the sun and not vice versa. A group of radical theologians have argued for another 'Copernican revolution' to take place, not in the world of cosmological theory, but in the world of religion. God, they say, is at the centre, and all the religions revolve around him. Jesus is not 'the' saviour of the world: he is but one of a number of saviours. Sadly, in today's multi-racial and multi-faith Britain many have accepted this kind of argument. The idea of Christians going overseas with the good news of Jesus therefore seems a nonsense.

But the truth is otherwise. For Jesus said: 'I am the way, and the truth, and the life. No one comes to the Father except through me' (John 14:6). He is the only way to God.

To believe that all religions lead to God is a piece of illogical and sentimental nonsense. The fact is that the religions of the world are extremely diverse. As long ago as 1890, the great pioneer in comparative religion Sir James Frazer stated: 'there is probably no subject in the world about which opinions differ so much as the nature of religion, and to frame a definition of it which would satisfy everyone must obviously be impossible'. In the light of this diversity, it just doesn't make sense to believe that they all lead to God. It's like saying that any road from any town in Britain will lead to London, whereas in fact many a road leads anywhere but to London. Similarly, there is only one route to God, and that is through Jesus. All the other routes or religions fail to lead people to God.

It is important to remember that from the beginning the Christian faith has been an exclusive faith. Multi-faith is not a new phenomenon to which the church has to adapt.

Paul, for instance, spoke of many 'gods' and 'lords': 'Yet for us there is one God, the Father, from whom are all things and for whom we exist; and one Lord, Jesus Christ, through whom are all things and through whom we exist' (1 Corinthians 8:6). The first Christians were quite sure that Jesus was the only way to God. Peter said to the highest Jewish council of the land: 'There is salvation in no one else, for there is no other name under heaven given among mortals by which we must be saved' (Acts 4:12).

Why are Christians so sure that Jesus is the only way to God? First of all, because of who he was. Jesus claimed to be the Son of God. In this respect the Christian faith is totally different from other religions. C. S. Lewis wrote:

> If you had gone to Buddha and asked him 'Are you the son of Brahma?' he would have said: 'my son, you are still in the vale of illusion'. If you had gone to Socrates and asked, 'Are you Zeus?' he would have laughed at you. If you had gone to Mohammed and asked, 'Are you Allah?' he would first have rent his clothes and then cut your head off.

Similarly, no other religious teacher ever claimed to be the way. Buddha, for example, when he was dying, told followers not to remember him, but his teaching. But Jesus never said: 'Follow my teaching'; he said: 'Follow me.' Only the Son of God could make such a claim.

Secondly, Jesus is the only way because of what he has done. Other religions point to humanity's thirst for God, whereas Jesus has dealt with our thirst by dealing with the barrier separating us from God. For that which separates us from God is not our lack of knowledge, but rather our sin. Jesus has broken down that barrier. The death of Jesus was no unfortunate accident when a gifted young religious teacher met an unhappy end; rather, it was the moment when Jesus, the Son of God, offered himself as a sacrifice to take away the sin of the world.

By contrast with other religions, the Christian gospel is about 'news', and not 'views'. It centres on an event that has taken place within time and space. God has intervened in human history. Through his Son he has entered our world and on the cross dealt with our sin. No other religion can deal with this basic problem of existence. This is why Jesus is the one and only way to God. This too is why we need to take the news of Jesus to 'the ends of the earth' (Acts 1:8).

Scriptures to reflect on

- 'For God so loved the world that he gave his only Son, so that everyone who believes in him may not perish but may have eternal life' (John 3:16).
- 'We know that this is truly the Saviour of the world' (John 4:42).
- 'You will be my witnesses in Jerusalem, in all Judea and Samaria, and to the ends of the earth' (Acts 1:8).
- 'In Christ God was reconciling the world to himself' (2 Corinthians 5:19).
- 'God our Saviour ... desires everyone to be saved and to come to the knowledge of the truth. For there is one God; there is also one mediator between God and humankind' (1 Timothy 2:3–4).

34. Give money away

An issue we face as a church is the amount of money we should give away. In theory we operate an 'all-in-budget', which includes not just the money we plan to spend on our own mission and ministry, but also the money we plan to give away to such causes as Home Mission and the Baptist Missionary Society. The reality, however, is that there are a host of other occasions when money is raised for outside projects.

For example, we have love offerings at Christmas (last year we gave to a new hospice for young adults, which one of our members is hoping to start up) and at Harvest (this year we are giving to development work in Afghanistan sponsored by BMS). As part of a townwide project, every September we send boxes of food to Eastern Europe; and in November we send personal gifts in shoe boxes to an operation run by Samaritan's Purse. We also raise yet further money through a Bible-a-month scheme promoted by the Bible Society, a missionary birthday scheme promoted by the BMS, and there is personalized missionary support for individuals connected with the church. And then all the tips from our Oasis café go to a different monthly good cause. Add too, the money that comes in for Tearfund in March, and Christian Aid in May, and the sums of money for charity that are raised through donations at funerals in lieu of flowers, then we are giving away huge amounts.

A major contention, however, is the proportion of money we should give away (my understanding is that this is an issue in other churches too). For some people the more money their church can give away, the better. But is that really so? After all, it is not as if the money retained is necessarily spent on ourselves. Surely, the money retained is used for mission in one's own locality, and that is no bad thing. For at its very lowest level, if churches fail to invest in mission at home, then in future there will be fewer people to give to mission beyond their town!

When I first came to Chelmsford, the church was giving away to outside causes 20% of all the money given to our all-in-budget. Then, as a result of committing ourselves to a major redevelopment project (which ended up costing the church £2 million, and on which we still owe around £275,000), not surprisingly, we found there was an impact on the general budget, with the result that we were able to give away only 10% of our income. There were howls of protest from certain quarters. 'God will not bless us if we give away only 10%,' said one irate middle-aged lady. 'On what basis do you make that judgment?', I wondered to myself. We now give away to outside causes 12% of money given to our all-in-budget – and as a result have put our own internal church budget under strain. Personally, I feel that churches can make a fetish of the percentage they give away. Furthermore, such calculations are often a nonsense – for they fail to take account of all the other money we give away. In our case, for instance, we are actually giving away at least 25% of our income – if not considerably more.[1]

A job description for a church treasurer

The church treasurer's responsibilities can be divided into two: (1) the marrying together of vision and financial resources by engendering enthusiasm for giving, developing innovative ways of increasing income, and preparing the church budget and accounts; (2) overseeing the work of the financial assistants appointed to care for and control the day-to-day income and expenditure of the church.

Scriptures to reflect on

- 'It is not right that we should neglect the word of God in order to wait at tables. Therefore, friends, select from among yourselves seven men of good standing, full of the Spirit and of wisdom, whom we may appoint to this task' (Acts 6:2–3).
- 'The disciples determined that according to their ability, each would send relief to the believers living in Judea; this they did, sending it to the elders by Barnabas and Saul' (Acts 11:29–30).
- 'Contribute to the needs of the saints' (Romans 12:13).
- 'It is a question of a fair balance between your present abundance and their need' (2 Corinthians 8:13–14).
- 'They [James, Cephas and John] asked only one thing, that we remember the poor, which was actually what I was eager to do' (Galatians 2:10).

Part 5: Leadership

35. Give the lead your church needs

Traditionally, ordination has been understood as the church conferring on its ministers the authority to preach the Word and to administer the Sacraments. But from a New Testament perspective this priestly emphasis on the role of the minister is misplaced. The New Testament emphasis is upon leadership. Paul, for instance, in 1 Corinthians 12 and Romans 12, as also in Ephesians 4, describes how all God's people are called to serve, but some are called to lead (see Romans 12:8; 1 Corinthians 12:8; Ephesians 4:7). Indeed, in the light of the New Testament I believe that first and foremost ordination is the act whereby the church confers authority upon its ministers.

Whatever the niceties of theological interpretation, one thing is certain: if today's churches are to face up today to the challenges offered by contemporary culture, then it desperately needs leaders who will think through those challenges and who will offer strategies for enabling their churches to fulfil Christ's mission today. If such strategies are to be effective, then churches will need leaders who will help enable churches to make the necessary changes to their life in order to adopt the necessary strategies.

Today's ministers need to be leaders. For where the right leaders are not only present, but also exercising their power to lead, there the church will grow and new members will be found. What is more, these new members will not just be Christians 'recycled' from other churches, but converts whose lives have truly been turned around by the gospel of Christ. But this will happen only as leaders exercise their 'powers' of leadership. Chaplains may have a role to play in hospitals and in prisons – they have, however, no role to play in the church. One reason why many churches are making little impact on their communities is that time and again their ministers have felt trapped by the personal needs and expectations of their members. They have assumed the role of their church's personal chaplain. But the fact is that there is more to ministry in the local church than caring for the pastoral needs of church people – ministry also involves caring for those outside the church. Ordination to the Christian ministry places a call on ministers to mobilize their people for ministry and mission not only in the church, but also beyond the confines of the church.

In practical terms this means that, first of all, ministers must exercise the power that is theirs and give the lead their churches need. As Peter Wagner, the American church-growth guru, somewhat proactively once said: 'Pastor, you should be the spark plug! Pastor don't be afraid of your power!' Yes, it can be uncomfortable being a leader – the person first out of the trench is first in the firing line. Secondly, this means that churches should encourage their pastors to give a lead – and unless it truly is an act of *kamikazi*, they should more often follow rather than question it. One thing is for sure: the church that forever quibbles over its leader's proposals is doomed to stagnation and to death.[1]

The power of self-control

Paul in his injunction to Timothy to 'rekindle the gift of God that is within you' links the exercise of power with 'love' and with 'self-control' or 'self-discipline' (2 Timothy 1:6). I am reminded of the third beatitude in the Sermon on the Mount. Jesus said: 'Blessed are the meek, for they will inherit the earth' (Matthew 5:5). It is possible that the original words of Jesus in Aramaic referred back to the Hebrew text of Psalm 37:11, where the reference is to the *ănāwîm*, the ordinary term for the 'poor' and the 'afflicted'. On the other hand, the beatitude as we now have it in Matthew's Gospel reflects the Septuagint version of Psalm 37:11, where the psalmist speaks of the 'meek' (*praeis*). In common Greek usage the 'meek' were not weaklings, but rather the strong whose power was under control. Aristotle, for instance, defined the meek person as one who is 'neither too hasty nor too slow-tempered. He does not become angry with those he ought not to, nor fail to become angry with whom he ought.'[2] Meekness on Aristotle's definition is gentleness combined with strength.

Jesus in the so-called 'Great Invitation' invited would-be disciples to take on his yoke and learn from him 'for I am meek and humble in heart' (Matthew 11:29, Authorized Version), and in so doing combines the idea of gentleness with strength. For Jesus is here inviting others to experience God's love and power as they live their life in fellowship with himself. It was by this 'meekness' and 'gentleness' of Christ that Paul later appealed to the unruly Corinthians for sympathy and obedience (2 Corinthians 10:1).

When Jesus rode into Jerusalem on a donkey he deliberately pointed to an Old Testament prophecy in which the expected Messiah was described in terms of 'meekness' (Zechariah 9:9). As the time when he cleansed the temple indicated, Jesus was no weakling; and yet as his encounter with the woman caught in adultery showed, he could be gentle. His passions were under control.

As Graham Kendrick, the modern Christian songwriter, so well expressed it, in Jesus we see both 'meekness and majesty'.

All this is relevant to Christian leaders. Where power and love and self-control are combined, there 'meekness/gentleness' is found. Such a spirit is to characterize the way in which discipline is exercised (Galatians 6:1) as also the way in which opposition is met (2 Timothy 2:25). God does not want spineless leaders; he wants leaders who are able to speak the truth in love, leaders whose lives exhibit the power of self-control.

Scriptures to reflect on

- Jesus 'appointed twelve . . . to have authority to cast out demons' (Mark 3:14–15).
- 'Whoever wishes to become great among you must be your servant' (Mark 10:43).

- 'Respect those who labour among you, and have charge of you in the Lord and admonish you' (1 Thessalonians 5:12).
- 'God did not give us a spirit of cowardice, but rather a spirit of power and of love and of self-discipline' (2 Timothy 1:7).
- 'Do not lord it over those in your charge, but be examples to the flock' (1 Peter 5:3).

36. Communicate effectively with your flock

As a young minister I once wrote an article for a national Christian monthly in which I strongly urged my readers to 'scrap the church magazine'. 'Church magazines', I said, 'are a waste of good paper – plus a good deal of time and effort.' I went on to argue that it was a waste of time giving news in a church magazine, because by the time the magazine was published, the news would be old, and 'old news doesn't work'. Instead, of a church magazine, I said, produce a weekly news bulletin. And as a man who practised what he preached, I encouraged my then church to scrap its monthly magazine and instead put all its energies into the production of a weekly news bulletin.

But twenty years later I find that I have changed my mind. A major reason for this change of mind is that patterns of churchgoing have changed. People, for instance, are no longer so regular in their church attendance. Twenty years ago 'twicers' were people who attended church morning and evening; today 'twicers' are people who attend twice a month. With increased affluence as well as increased holiday allowance, people are forever away, either on holiday or simply visiting friends and relations. It is therefore increasingly difficult on any given Sunday for ministers to address a particular message to the church. Indeed, in our church it now takes us three Sundays to get over a message to the church as a whole. It is at this point that a monthly church magazine has a vital role to play, for through their monthly 'letters' ministers speak to the church as a whole.

I confess that at one stage I simply used to dash off the briefest of letters. Now, however, conscious of the strategic value of the magazine, I take a good deal more effort, as I consider what particular issue is best to raise with my readers. Likewise, because of the changed pattern of church attendance, the church magazine becomes an important medium of news. True, the news it contains may not be the latest – but unless news is repeated three weeks running in the weekly news bulletin (and interestingly, I know of one church that does precisely that), a good deal of people miss out if news is confined to the weekly news bulletin.

Another important feature of our church magazine is the church diary, which this month covered five sides. In our church (and no doubt many others) there is so much going on in a month that there is no way in which it can be dealt with in a weekly news bulletin. Then, of course, there are all the other features: financial updates, missionary letters, reports from various organizations, expressions of views of one kind or another.

Yes, the church magazine has a very real role to play – and the fact that so many are willing to pay for a copy is an indication of its felt value.[1]

Communications within the church

To what extent do internal communications feature on your church's agenda? Some years ago we created a 'media team' within our church, with the aim 'to help everyone understand what is happening within the fellowship and to tell the people of Chelmsford where we are and what we're about'. Communication within the church is just as important as communication without – indeed, the larger the church, the more important internal communication is.

There are a number of ways in which church members can communicate with one another. The Sunday notices are one key means, although care must be taken that the church is not overloaded with information, for otherwise people will switch off. The weekly news-sheet is another vital means of communication. So too are leaflets, posters and displays.

Some churches use e-mail as the main channel of communication and have replaced the weekly newsletter with a weekly e-mail. This is fine where the congregation is predominantly young and where therefore everybody has e-mail facilities. In our church, for instance, youth groups e-mail or text all their members on a regular basis. Likewise, when I want to communicate with my deacons, I e-mail them. However, most older people are still not on the Net, with the result that one cannot rely on e-mails to communicate to all and sundry.

Once or twice a year I tend to send a personal pastoral letter to all members and friends of the church. Sometimes I have done this at the beginning of the year and have included the church's new motto card. I always send out a letter just before the church anniversary, with information about the church's annual thank-offering together with an envelope for gifts.

A more confidential means of communicating to the church is the church meeting. Within the semi-privacy of such a meeting I am able to speak about some of the more sensitive pastoral issues, which could not be shared on a Sunday. On one such occasion I gave news of a marriage breakdown and asked the church for its prayerful support of the couple; on another occasion I informed the church that one of our younger members was expecting a baby out of wedlock and asked the church to refrain from gossip but rather to provide support.

However, the main means of communication remains the church magazine. It is important to stress that the church magazine is not in the business of seeking to be a pale reflection of other Christian magazines on the market. The stated purpose of our church magazine, for instance, is to enable the church to fulfil its mission better of 'going Christ's way and making disciples'. In particular, this means that our magazine is there to serve the overall ministry aims of our church; namely: 'exciting fresh hope and faith in God; embracing "love of another kind"; encouraging personal change and growth; and empowering for witness and service'. This means, for instance, that the magazine is not a place for individual members to present views at variance with the overall direction of the church's leadership. The concept of editorial freedom in this regard does not exist! The magazine is there to serve the interests of the church.

Communication has a vital role to play in every church. Needless to say, communication takes effort – not least effort to ensure that what is said is actually heard and understood. In the words of Max Warren, a former General Secretary of the Church Missionary Society, effective communication calls for 'quadruple-think'; that is, 'thinking over what I have to say: then thinking out how the other man will understand what I say: and then rethinking what I have to say: so that, when I say it, he will think what I am thinking!'[2]

Scriptures to reflect on
- 'Like cold water to a thirsty soul, / so is good news from a far country' (Proverbs 25:25).
- 'I have written to you rather boldly by way of reminder, because of the grace given me by God to be a minister of Christ Jesus' (Romans 15:15–16).
- 'They called the church together and related all that God had done with them' (Acts 14:27).
- 'Whatever is true, whatever is honourable, whatever is just, whatever is pure, whatever is pleasing, whatever is commendable, if there is any excellence and if there is anything worthy of praise, think about these things' (Philippians 4:8).
- 'Let anyone who has an ear listen to what the Spirit is saying to the churches' (Revelation 2:7).

3**7.** Develop a prayer strategy

In years gone by, the midweek prayer meeting was at the heart of the church's life and was viewed as the 'powerhouse' of the church. Today things have changed. In most churches centralized midweek meetings of any kind, let alone prayer meetings, appear to be unpopular. Instead, we have home groups (or fellowship groups, cell groups, or whatever is the preferred name for your church's small groups). And there, of course, people pray. First and foremost they pray for one another – and rightly so. Unfortunately, that is sometimes as far as the prayer goes. The concerns of the wider church somehow go by the board. However, to be fair, that is not always true. My mind goes to two long-running small groups in our church that have only one purpose: to pray for the church and its ministers. As a minister, I feel truly privileged.

But important though they are, these are just small groups. So, from time to time, at the beginning of a new session, for instance, we cancel our home groups and organize a so-called 'church-wide' prayer meeting – but far fewer people turn up to the central meeting than would have been present in the home groups.

Another place for prayer is our midweek church meeting, held five times a year (the remaining church meetings are held after the

Sunday morning service and are therefore necessarily short); there we devote the first half of the meeting to a brief act of opening worship, the sharing of news and concerns, and prayer. The difficulty here is that in this larger setting only the confident few feel free to pray aloud – so I tend to use 'bidding' prayers, where people do the praying in their hearts.

In addition to all this praying, one must not forget that, without exception, all the organizations and activities of the church have their own times of praying. Indeed, in addition to their times of regular praying, some of these organizations come together for a Saturday morning of prayer. For instance, all the organizations involved in youth ministry meet once a year for corporate prayer, as also all the organizations involved in ministry to seniors.

I sometimes wonder whether those who hanker after the old-fashioned midweek prayer meeting are mindful of what goes on. The chief place, however, for large-scale corporate prayer is surely the Sunday services. In our church the Sunday intercessory prayers are serious business. The instructions that go out to those church members tasked with this responsibility is that they lead us in three or four short prayers to be focused on aspects relating to the church (local or overseas), the nation (or local community) and the world. Then, after the service, prayer ministry is offered for individuals in need of one kind or another. In other words, although we have no midweek prayer meeting, this does not mean that the church does not pray. And I am sure that what is true of our church is true of many others too. So perhaps we should not be too concerned at the demise of the old midweek prayer meeting.[1]

Small groups – the heart of the church's prayer life?

Jesus said: 'If two of you agree on earth about anything you ask, it will be done for you by my Father in heaven. For where two or three are gathered in my name, I am there among them' (Matthew 18:19–20). No doubt we can quite legitimately apply this to the twenties and the thirties, the two hundreds and the three hundreds, and even the two thousands and the three thousands. However, in the first instance this was spoken of a small group of two or three people, and so gives particular encouragement to the creation of small groups for prayer. The advantages of such groups are several.

Firstly, it is here that the new Christian may learn to pray. All too often we have expected new Christians to grow on their own in the Christian life. Yet we ask this of no ordinary child; for children, the family is where the learning process begins. This is particularly applicable to prayer. It is not enough for prayer to be part of the syllabus of a discipleship class; what is needed is 'on-the-job training', the experience of a small praying group. In the end, prayer is not taught, but 'caught'.

Secondly, it is in the small group that many busy young mothers have been helped to pray. Whether we like it or not, there are many mothers with young children who find it difficult to establish a Quiet Time of their own. This is especially true of those who have non-Christian husbands. For them the weekly small prayer group is a spiritual lifeline.

Thirdly, it is in the small group that Christians in general can develop in their Christian life. We have all so much further to go along the path of prayer. In the meeting with others our prayer life receives stimulus and encouragement.

Fourthly, in the small group all may participate. The large group inhibits, whereas confidence is quickly gained in the small group – particularly where the small group is only three or four in number.

Fifthly, it is in such small groups for prayer that the joys and problems of the Christian life are shared. In the large group prayers tend to be abstract and impersonal, whereas in the small group prayers can become concrete and personal. Instead of just praying for 'them', we begin to pray for 'us'. It is at that stage that prayer becomes real and vital for many.

Small groups, not the traditional midweek meeting, are at the heart of the church's prayer life. It is there that we can bear one another's burdens (Galatians 6:2), sorrow and rejoice together (1 Corinthians 12:26), and truly pray for one another (see James 5:16). In the words of George Whitefield:

> My brethren, let us plainly and freely tell one another what God has done for our souls. To this end you would do well ... to form yourselves into little companies of four or five each, and meet once a week to tell each other what is in your hearts: that you may then pray for and comfort each other as need shall require. None but those who

have experienced it can tell the unspeakable advantages of such a union and communion of souls ... None I think that truly loves his own soul and his brethren as himself, will be shy of opening his heart, in order to have their advice, reproof, admonition and prayer, as occasion requires. A sincere person will esteem it one of the greatest blessings.

Scriptures to reflect on

- 'Have faith in God ... I tell you, whatever you ask for in prayer, believe that you have received, and it will be yours' (Mark 11:22, 24).
- 'If you abide in me, and my words abide in you, ask for whatever you wish, and it will be done for you' (John 15:7).
- 'They devoted themselves to the apostles' teaching and fellowship, to the breaking of bread and the prayers' (Acts 2:42).
- 'Pray in the Spirit at all times in every prayer and supplication. To that end keep alert and always persevere in prayer for all the saints' (Ephesians 6:18).
- 'You do not have, because you do not ask' (James 4:2).

38. Appoint leaders

Today many Baptist churches have appointed elders as well as elected deacons on the ground that this is the pattern for church life laid down in Scripture. But although this was the pattern operating in the churches of Ephesus for which Timothy was responsible (see 1 Timothy 3:1–13), it was by no means the universal pattern. The fact is that the church at Jerusalem was structured differently from the church at Corinth, and the church at Corinth was structured differently from the church at Ephesus. There is no one scriptural pattern for leadership. Furthermore, to complicate matters, we have no sure knowledge of the precise role deacons played over against elders at Ephesus. When he wrote to Timothy, Paul was far more interested in the qualities necessary for deacons as distinct from their duties. However, a Baptist tradition has developed whereby elders are seen to have a leadership role in the spiritual and pastoral affairs of the church, while the deacons are seen as responsible for the more practical tasks. This Baptist tradition, however, has some serious drawbacks.

First of all, it is not always easy to distinguish between the spiritual and the practical. The handling of money, for instance, normally seen as a 'practical' task, actually calls for a high degree of spirituality.

Many a pastor has reason to thank God for a godly church treasurer, endued with the spiritual gift of wisdom.

Secondly, this distinction between the spiritual and the practical almost always leads to connotations of first- and second-class leaders (for the former are inevitably viewed as more spiritual than the latter).

Thirdly, there is a tendency for elders to be in the same mould as their pastor – indeed, often the elders are chosen by the pastor. The result is that elders often fail to complement their pastor.

Fourthly, the introduction of elders into our churches appears to me to be a throwback to a past culture and smacks of irrelevancy today. Certainly, the term 'elders' is positively quaint, if not ludicrous, when applied today to middle-aged men (and they do tend to be men). However, in Paul's day there was no such thing as middle age: in Roman society, for instance, a man was called a young man (literally a 'juvenile', *iuvenis*) when he was under forty, and an 'old man' (*senex* – the word from which we get 'senile'!) when he was 40 or over.

My own preferred option is to have one leadership team (yes, let's do away with the diaconate – that too belongs to a past era) who serve their Lord and his church by giving direction to the church in its ministry and mission. Accountable to the leadership team and through the leadership team are then a number of small task-oriented teams with responsibility for overseeing and developing clearly defined areas of the church's life, such as social action and evangelism, nurture and development, pastoral care, and areas such as finance and fabric. But let's not have elders – leadership becomes too complicated![1]

Defining leadership

Leadership is the key priority in the churches of today. Preaching is important, worship is important, pastoral care, evangelism and social action – all these things must come high on the agenda. But uppermost comes leadership. Many churches are dying for lack of leadership; while others are being split asunder for lack of leadership.

But what precisely is leadership? Harry Truman, a former American president, said: 'A leader is a person who has the ability to get others to do what they don't want to do, and to like it' – but that sounds like manipulation! Mahatma Ghandi identified tenacity as the key element: 'to put up with misrepresentation and to stick to one's guns come what may – this is the essence of leadership'. Hannibal, as he contemplated crossing the Alps, typified this attitude: 'I will find a way or make one.' Napoleon defined a leader as 'a dealer in hope'; whereas the ancient Chinese philosopher Lao-tse said: 'A leader is best when people barely know he exists.'

My preferred definition of leadership is that advocated by John Adair, a distinguished British leadership development consultant, who wrote of the good leader as one who 'works as a senior partner with other members to achieve the task, build the team, and meet individual needs'.[2] Translated into language associated with the Christian church, 'the other members' with whom the pastor as 'senior partner' works are the leaders of the church. Together the leaders face three challenges:

1. *Achieving the task.* Within a Christian frame of reference, the task is the mission of the church. This mission might be interpreted in large general terms relating to the overall implementation of the Great Commission. On the other hand, the mission might be interpreted in more specific terms, relating to the particular mission of a local church in a given area at a given time.

Needless to say, before the task may be achieved, it must first be defined. Such a defining of the task involves the leaders putting before the church a vision of what God is calling his people to be and do. Many churches find it helpful in this respect to develop a mission statement for the church's life together. For example, on the basis of the Great Commission as found in Matthew 28:18–20 and John 20:21 a church might state: 'Our mission is to go Christ's way and make disciples.' However, mission statements by themselves are of limited value. Aims and objectives need to be developed, along with appropriate strategies. This is the task of leadership. Of course, these aims and objectives and strategies will need to be accepted and owned by the church meeting – but the task of leadership is enabling the church meeting to grasp the vision.

2. *Building the team.* Within a Christian frame of reference the church is the team. What's more, the church is a team with a task. Every-member-ministry is suddenly given direction. There is a common goal to which all can work. The task of leaders within the

church is continually to seek to weld the team together by giving it a sense of common purpose and direction. When relationship difficulties arise, then leaders must be prepared to deal with such difficulties. For healing and harmony to prevail, this may involve confronting those who need to be confronted. At other times leaders may need to act as peace-brokers and go-betweens. 'Teamsmanship' (the art of becoming a team-player) must constantly be worked at. Leaders have a particular responsibility to make 'every effort to maintain the unity of the Spirit in the bond of peace' (Ephesians 4:3).

3. *Meeting the needs of individuals.* If members of the team are to work effectively as they seek to achieve the task, then their individual needs have to be met. What are these needs? It seems to me that they are fivefold: church members need to (1) be led in worship, (2) be taught, (3) receive pastoral care, (4) experience fellowship, and (5) find avenues of service. The task of leaders is to ensure that all these needs are met. It is as these basic needs are met that members are equipped 'for the work of ministry' (Ephesians 4:12).

Scriptures to reflect on

- 'You know that among the Gentiles those whom they recognize as their rulers lord it over them, and their great ones are tyrants over them. But it is not so among you; but whoever wishes to become great among you must be your servant' (Mark 10:42–43).
- 'Jesus . . . tied a towel around himself . . . and began to wash his disciples' feet . . . "I have set you an example, that you also should do as I have done to you"' (John 13:3, 5, 15).
- 'Select from among yourselves seven men of good standing, full of the Spirit and of wisdom' (Acts 6:3).
- 'We have gifts that differ according to the grace given to us: . . . the leader, in diligence' (Revised English Bible: 'If you are a leader, lead with enthusiasm') (Romans 12:6, 8).
- 'Obey your leaders and submit to them, for they are keeping watch over your souls and will give an account' (Hebrews 13:17).

39. Build teams

As churches grow, ministry teams of one kind or another come into being. Not all the members of these teams may be paid, nor are they necessarily all full-time. But one thing is for sure: they form a team. Indeed, it has been said: 'two's a company, three's a team, and more than fifteen's a crowd'.

For the sake of good relationships it is important that the members of the team adopt a set of team values. In our church we have adopted the following guidelines to help us move forward in our life together:

- *Mutual care.* We will model the kinds of relationships that ideally should characterize the life of the church in general. We will love one another, pray for one another, honour one another, care for one another, encourage one another, and speak the truth in love to one another. We will be there for one another, come hell or high water.
- *Communication.* We will keep one another informed of what we are doing – and of what we are hoping to do. We will therefore come to our team meetings ready to share.

- *Openness.* We will be open with one another. There may be times when the ministers will not be free to be open with the rest of the team; however, there is no place for ministers to keep secrets from one another. A confidence does not necessarily mean that we cannot share information with one another.
- *Honesty.* In our thoughts and our feelings we will be honest with one another. If something has upset us, then we will surface it, recognizing that 'today's niggle could be tomorrow's resentment, and next week's breakdown'.
- *Loyalty.* Outside our team meeting, we will always stand up for one another. While none of us is perfect, and there will be times when we make a mess of things, we will resist the temptation of criticizing one another to other members. The place for criticism is either one to one or in the team meeting.
- *Positivity.* In our relationships with one another (and indeed with the rest of the church) we will always exude a positive spirit. We will shun negative talking and thinking. We will instead affirm one another and will speak well of one another.
- *Excellence.* We will never be satisfied with the second best. In our desire for excellence we will foster a healthy dissatisfaction with the way things are and will always strive for better.
- *Faith.* We will strengthen one another's hope and faith in God, and we will foster each other's passion for Christ. We will be bold in the way we develop our various ministries – and where there are failures, we will help one another to learn and then to use the failure as a stepping board for fresh advances.[1]

Work more generally at creating teams

Our church is big on teams. In addition to the 'ministry team' composed of the ministers and others working for the church, which meets together on a formal basis once a week, there is also the leadership team, composed of the ministers and deacons, which meets monthly and oversees the church's mission and ministry.

Then there are ten task-oriented teams, normally led by deacons and accountable to the leadership team (and ultimately to the church meeting). These teams tend to meet every six to eight weeks. They have responsibility for overseeing and developing clearly defined areas of the church's mission and ministry; namely, social action, evangelism, nurture and development, pastoral, youth and children's ministry, ministry to seniors, mission beyond Chelmsford, worship, fabric, finance and media. The teams themselves are small in size and do not normally number more than seven members. The mandate of the team members is not to do all the work themselves, but to empower and encourage others in the church to get behind whatever may be their particular project.

The church itself may also be likened to a team. True, it is a challenge to ensure that every member is engaged in appropriate ministry. In a large church it is more easily possible for members to behave like passengers rather than active members of the crew. But where a church is broken down into small groups, then 'every-member-ministry' becomes feasible. One of the key tasks of a pastor in this context is that of welding together what may appear initially to be a motley crew, each doing his or her own thing, into a team, working together to fulfil the mission of the church. Such a welding together is not easy. Furthermore, the larger a church, the more difficult the welding together becomes. And yet it can be done – through the Sunday services, the monthly church meetings, and written forms of communication such as the monthly church magazine.

Whether or not we are justified in calling all these different groups 'teams' is debatable. Indeed, it is said that any group of over twelve members is no longer a group, but a meeting. Certainly, the larger a group, the more relationships need to be formed. It has been estimated that 'members of a group of six have 15 relationships with which they must deal to interact as a group. A group of eight persons has 28 potential relationships; a group of 10 has 45; a group of 15 has 105; and a group of 20 has the staggering possibility of 190 relation-ships.'[2] Research in group dynamics suggests that eight members may in fact be the optimum figure for the size of a team. If this is true, then those churches that have modelled their leadership teams on the number of so-called 'deacons' (seven!) found in Acts 6 are in fact on to a good thing.

Scriptures to reflect on
- 'He [Jesus] appointed twelve, whom he also named apostles, to be with him . . . ' (Mark 3:14).

- 'They chose Stephen, a man full of faith and the Holy Spirit, together with Philip, Prochorus, Nicanor, Timon, Parmenas, and Nicolaus . . . ' (Acts 6:5).
- 'Paul and Timothy, servants of Christ Jesus, To all the saints in Christ Jesus who are in Philippi, with the bishops and deacons' (Philippians 1:1).
- 'Let each of you look not to your own interests, but to the interests of others' (Philippians 2:4).
- 'May the Lord make you increase and abound in love for one another and for all' (1 Thessalonians 3:12).

40. Encourage volunteers

In many (if not most) work situations in Britain, annual appraisals have become a way of life. Once a year employees have an opportunity on an individual basis to sit down with their immediate superior and review their past performance with a view to setting fresh goals for the following year. As many of you will know, first and foremost, appraisal is intended to be a positive process. If appraisal involves criticism, then it is constructive criticism with the well-being of the individual as well as the well-being of the organization in mind.

It is my conviction that appraisals should be a way of life for all pastors – not least because it helps us to be better ministers. But why should appraisal be limited just to the church's ministers? For are not all God's people called to the work of ministry? Surely as Baptists we believe in 'the ministry of all and the leadership of some'? Theologically speaking, our membership rolls are in fact 'ministry rolls'.

When we lay hands on and pray for the newly baptized, we are not simply seeking God's blessing on their lives – we are also in effect commissioning them for service. For this reason some theologians liken this ceremony to a lay form of ordination. So, when I give new members the right hand of fellowship and welcome them into our church, I ask them this question: 'Do you commit yourself to love and serve the Lord within this fellowship as within the wider world?' Commitment to Christ involves commitment to his service, and 'service', of course, is just another word for 'ministry'.

To give expression to this concept of every-member-ministry I sometimes wonder whether churches should put something along the lines of the following on their noticeboards: 'Leader: Rev. Joe Bloggs. Ministers: All of us.'

If then, we are all in the business of 'ministry', then (in theory at least) we should all be willing to be appraised from time to time, with a view to, on the one hand receiving encouragement, and on the other hand, receiving help in setting new goals for the next period of ministry.

The thought is not as novel as it may sound. Some time ago I read of an Anglican vicar in an inner-city Liverpool church, who drew up an individual contract of a year with each of his members, with a mandatory review after three months. This contract included the individual's prayer discipline, personal family relationships, areas of work related to personal gifts, and suggestions for further study and conferences. Here indeed was an example of pastoral visiting with a difference!

If such a wide-ranging contract with every church member appears to be too demanding, then what about devising simple job specifications for every volunteer in the church – and then ensuring that there is some kind of annual review, even if it is no more than an informal discussion between the volunteer and the volunteer's 'supervisor'? What a difference this could make to Sunday school teachers, for instance, whose service is all too often taken for granted. Yes, such appraisals take time and effort – but if they result in better motivated volunteers, then surely such time and effort is worthwhile.[1]

Say thank you

I have just come from a splendid three-course lunch, including coffee, which was held in a local further education college, where trainee restaurant and hotel staff cooked and waited on us. It was 'silver service' and white table cloths. It felt a really special occasion, and we took over two and a half hours over the various courses. To this lunch we had invited all the volunteers who help with our church centre during the day. They paid for their drinks, and the church paid for their meal. Although £10 per head, we felt it to be a great investment. It was our way of saying thank you to a group of key volunteers in the church.

The previous week my wife and I had put on a supper party in our home for our leadership team and their partners. With thirty guests, there was no way in which we could all sit down around one table. Instead, it had to be a buffet supper – but none the worse for that. Again, it was our way of saying thank you to our leaders.

Next month the lay leader of our pastoral team is putting on a buffet supper party in her home for all those involved in pastoral care in the church. Again, it is a way of saying thank you to all those helping with pastoral visiting.

But there are other ways of saying thank you to volunteers. In a month's time, at a morning service, I will be handing out 'long-service awards' to all those volunteers who have helped with our child-contact centre for over seven years. Not so long ago I did something similar with Sunday school teachers and helpers, but on that occasion it involved volunteers of five years' standing or more. This form of public recognition heightens the profile of the activity – and also enables us as a church to express our appreciation to all those who have helped over the years.

Another way of saying thank you is to do so with flowers. When there has been a wedding with lots of flowers to distribute after-wards, I often send bunches of flowers to volunteers as an expression of the church's appreciation.

And, of course, one can always write a letter. Every time a deacon comes to the end of a term of service, I always send a thank-you letter. It may sound somewhat formal, but these formalities are appreciated.

'Thank you' is one of the most important phrases in the English language.

Scriptures to reflect on
- 'You are those who have stood by me in my trials' (Luke 22:28).
- 'Outdo one another in showing honour' (Romans 12:10).

- 'Greet Prisca and Aquila, who work with me in Christ Jesus . . . to whom not only I give thanks, but also all the churches of the Gentiles' (Romans 16:3–4).
- 'I rejoice at the coming of Stephanas and Fortunatus and Achaicus . . . for they refreshed my spirit as well as yours. So give recognition to such people' (1 Corinthians 16:17–18).
- 'I thank my God . . . because of your sharing in the gospel . . .' (Philippians 1:3, 5).

41. Invest in buildings, invest in mission

We spent almost £2 million on redeveloping our church and as a result have ended up with a wonderful set of premises. But were we right or wrong to spend such a huge sum?

Some told us that we were wrong to spend that kind of money on ourselves. We should have given the money away to help smaller churches here at home or to the poor of the world. But that criticism is fundamentally flawed. We did not spend the money on 'ourselves': we invested the money in mission, and in particular in a mission facility appropriate to the new millennium.

The fact is that people's expectations have changed. The cinemas discovered that some years ago. They realized if they were to attract people to see their films, then it wasn't simply a matter of having good films to show. It was also a matter of having comfortable seats in which to watch the films. So they knocked down their old 'flea pits' and built new cinemas instead, with the result that people now go to the cinema again.

The parallel with church is clear. People are not prepared to put up with hard, uncomfortable pews, or with ill-heated and draughty buildings. What was good enough for their grandparents is no longer good enough for them. Just as the cinemas needed to upgrade their facilities to attract a new cinema-going public, so we churches, if we want to attract a new churchgoing public, must do the same.

Some critics have been more radical and have questioned whether we need a building at all. After all, Christians didn't have buildings until around AD 200. Our experience of having worshipped in a school for some nineteen months is that there are real disadvantages in renting other people's premises. Setting up for services was enormously time-demanding. And a school hall is not the most uplifting of environments in which to worship God. And as for all the other activities we ran during the week, it was a nightmare relocating our two mental-health clubs, our child-contact centre, and all the other activities one might expect of a busy church. It is difficult to engage in holistic mission without a building. Home groups have a role to play, not least in the area of enhancing and deepening fellowship, but they have their limitations when it comes to worship, evangelism and social service. Furthermore, the life expectancy of churches that do not have buildings of their own tends to be much shorter than those that do invest in bricks and mortar. It is actually good stewardship to invest in church buildings.

It is true that buildings are not essential to the being of the church. The church is people, not buildings. The temple at Jerusalem was replaced by the body of Christ. People therefore come first; buildings are only secondary. But buildings can serve the people of God. They can serve the people of God, not least in providing them with a base for worship and for mission. Buildings are a good investment in mission.[1]

Don't underestimate sacred symbols

Just as the love of God was expressed in human form, so too we may express our love for God in wood and brick. And just as the physical acts of eating bread and drinking wine can be means of grace, so too can the physical attributes of a building be a means of grace to those who worship. With this idea of sacred space for the worship of God, let me take you on a quick tour of our new 'meeting place'.

Perhaps the first thing you will notice is that there is no pulpit. Often 'six feet above contradiction', the pulpit proved to be an unhelpful barrier between the preacher and the congregation. But we have a lectern – or should we call it a 'preaching desk'? For it is not just an insignificant stand on which to rest a Bible. It is a solid piece of furniture. Its very solidity symbolizes the importance we pay to the preaching of God's Word. As a church we offer all kinds of styles of worship and of music, but central to them all is the exposition of the Word of God.

Then there is the communion table, beautiful in its simplicity. It is no altar, yet it speaks of the body and blood of Christ offered up in sacrifice for us, once and for all. It is a table, and speaks of the fellowship we experience in Jesus when we come together around the table. It is an 'open' table, and speaks of the Lord's invitation to all who 'sincerely love our Lord Jesus Christ and desire to be his true disciples' to come, eat and drink. It is a constant reminder of the grace of God.

Behind the table, yet in clear view of all, is a wonderful see-through baptistery. If the table speaks of what Jesus has done for us, the baptistery speaks of the response we need to make to Jesus. Jesus invites us to make his death and his resurrection our own – to share with him in his death and burial, so that we might rise with him to newness of life. At the heart of our Baptist understanding of baptism is our theology of conversion. The baptistery symbolizes faith's response to the grace of God.

Either side of the baptistery are two magnificent banners. Rich in symbolism, they depict the triumphant words of Jesus 'I am the resurrection and the life'. Even those who fail to spot the symbolism of the lectern, the table and the baptistery, cannot fail to spot the symbols of the cross and resurrection. The crown of thorns and the crown of life are fairly obvious, but perhaps less so the purple robe of the Crucified and the catch of fish. But there may be other symbolism present too. Is the water issuing from the side of Christ symbolic of the Holy Spirit – or is it that the stake of the cross is plunged into the waters of chaos? Is the water swirling around the risen Lord symbolic of the river of the water of life of which we read in the book of Revelation? And what about the words 'I AM', a title for God, written above the cross – is the heart of God most clearly revealed in the cross?

To the west side of the baptistery is a large wooden cross. It is an empty cross, and not a crucifix – a reminder that our crucified Saviour is also the risen Lord.

To the east side of the baptistery are the drums and the piano, together with evidence of other instruments too. And of course there is our organ at the back. All these instruments symbolize our desire to worship God and give him the glory.

Around the platform area are chairs, arranged in one large semicircle. The importance of the chairs is not that we can be more comfortable – but that we can arrange them in such a way that we can see one another. When seated in ranks of pews, we saw only each others' backs – but now we can see the faces of at least some of our brothers and sisters.

And above us there is the high wooden roof with its imposing arches, reminding us of the wooden ark in which Noah and his family escaped from the flood, the ark that later became a symbol of the church, which in turn became a symbol of salvation. And, of course, there is the light streaming through the new roof lights. What a difference the light has made. It uplifts the spirit and inspires the soul. For us the light symbolizes the light of heaven – as the light of heaven streams in, we are reminded of Jacob's ladder stretching between heaven and earth, and of Jacob's discovery: 'This is . . . the house of God'; it is 'the gate of heaven' (Genesis 28:17).

When it came to rebuilding the chamber of the House of Commons, Winston Churchill said: 'We make our buildings and our buildings make us.' Sometimes we are the worse for the buildings we have built. With our remodelled 'meeting place' we are much the better able to worship God.

Scriptures to reflect on

- 'This is none other than the house of God, and this is the gate of heaven' (Genesis 28:17).
- 'Is it a time for you yourselves to live in your panelled houses, while this house lies in ruins? . . . build the house, so that I may take pleasure in it and be honoured' (Haggai 1:4, 8).
- 'This is my body . . . This is my blood of the covenant' (Mark 14:22, 24).
- 'He went to the synagogue on the sabbath day, as was his custom' (Luke 4:16).
- 'The Word became flesh' (John 1:14).

Part 6: Sunday services

42. Keep a balance in worship

Worship styles are changing. But then, has there ever been a period when worship styles have not changed? Some of the first Baptist worship services, for instance, lasted over three hours and included several sermons. Thank God we have moved on! The fact is that there is no one 'right' way to worship God.

As Baptists we may not be enamoured with the liturgical patterns of *Common Worship* – but this does not mean to say that our Baptist way of doing things is any more Spirit-inspired than that enjoyed by our Anglican brothers and sisters. And at any rate, what is 'our Baptist way' of worshipping God? With the sad demise of *Baptist Praise and Worship* we no longer have a common hymnbook – indeed, many a church has no hymnbook at all.

Of more concern than the lack of a common hymnbook, however, is the way in which in some churches the planning of worship is left to the last minute, as though spontaneity is a mark of spirituality. For me the reverse is the case: unprepared worship is a mark of laziness. God demands our best – not least in the area of worship. Good worship demands hard work and concentrated thought. Like King David, we should not offer God in worship that which costs us nothing (see 2 Samuel 24:24). Needless to say, a minister's preparation should not be a straitjacket – there are times when circumstances or just an inward sensing of the heart may dictate a change to the words we have chosen or the hymn we have chosen to sing. But these are the exceptions to the rule that Spirit-inspired worship is prepared worship.

As for the form of Spirit-inspired worship, that will vary: just as there are varieties of gifts, but the same Spirit, so there are varieties of Spirit-inspired worship forms. Just as there was no one pattern of worship in the early church (the worship at Corinth as described in 1 Corinthians 12 – 14 was undoubtedly very different from the worship at Ephesus, as outlined in Paul's letters to Timothy), so there is no one pattern of worship for today.

But although there may not be one basic order of service, there are a number of ingredients basic to worship. It has often been said that the essential ingredients of Spirit-inspired worship find their roots in the Jewish synagogue and the upper room. To the praise and prayer, the Scripture readings and the sermon (all characteristic of the Jewish synagogue), were added the breaking of bread and the fellowship of the upper room. In our Baptist churches today there is plenty of praise – but prayer in terms of intercessory prayer is often sadly missing; there is plenty of sermonizing, but sometimes very little Scripture; fellowship too is in good supply, but most Baptists celebrate the Lord's Supper just once a month (even where communion takes place once in the morning, and once in the evening, most people are not present at both services). Where a Baptist church has not got a fair balance of all these ingredients, then it seems to me that something is wrong. At the end of the day it is not the form but the content that counts.[1]

The essential ingredients of worship

Praise: The Jewish Talmud states: 'man should always first utter praise and then prayer'. This thought is possibly reflected in 1 Corinthians 14:26, where a hymn (literally, a 'psalm') heads the list of contributions. From Ephesians 5:18 and Colossians 3:16, with their reference to 'psalms, hymns, and spiritual songs', we may deduce that the early church knew variety in its worship right from the beginning. As many of the early Christian hymns and confessions preserved in the New Testament (e.g. Romans 1:3–4; Philippians 2:6–11; Colossians 1:15–20;

1 Timothy 3:16) attest, early Christian worship focused above all on the God who raised Jesus from the dead. Strangely, in many churches today Easter praise is limited to Easter day. How is it that the 'community of the resurrection', meeting on the first day of the week, fails to celebrate every Sunday God's triumph over sin and death?

Prayer: In the synagogue, praise moved into prayer with the 'Eighteen Blessings', which covered a wide variety of intercessions and petitions. Acts 2:41 suggests that, in Jerusalem at least, prayer was a hallmark of early Christian worship. Paul likewise expected the churches he pastored to take intercessory prayer seriously (1 Timothy 2:1–2). Unfortunately, in many of the less liturgical churches intercessory prayers at the main Sunday service are often noticeable by their absence; and where there are such prayers, they are often limited to the immediate needs of the fellowship. Similarly, prayers of confession are often absent, or if present are tacked on in a perfunctory manner; namely, 'and all these things we ask together with the forgiveness of our sins'.

Scripture: An essential ingredient of synagogue worship was the readings from the Law and the Prophets. 1 Timothy 4:13 indicates that the early church also made much of Scripture reading. For as Paul, with the Old Testament primarily in mind, says to Timothy: 'All scripture is inspired by God and is useful for teaching, for reproof, for correction, and for training in righteousness' (2 Timothy 3:16). Sadly, in all too many non-liturgical churches the diet of Scripture is severely limited.

Sermon: The Jews called their synagogues 'houses of instruction'. People gathered together to learn from the Word of God. After the Scriptures had been read, they were expounded. Likewise, teaching formed an essential element of early Christian worship (Acts 2:42; 1 Corinthians 14:26). As far as Paul was concerned, the role of pastor was synonymous with the role of teacher (Ephesians 4:11; see also 2 Timothy 4:1–5). Would that more Christians today took more seriously their need to learn from the Word of God. If they did, they would bring to church a personal copy of the textbook: their own Bible.

Breaking of bread: It was in the context of the upper room that Jesus broke bread, poured out wine and said: 'Do this in remembrance of me.' Ever since, the Lord's Supper has been a central act of Christian worship (see Acts 2:42; 20:7; 1 Corinthians 11:17–34). Alas, how complicated later theologians have made this act of remembrance!

Fellowship: In the early church the Last Supper was a fellowship meal, for when the first Christians broke bread, they broke bread within the context of a meal (see 1 Corinthians 11:17–34). However, it is probable that when Luke lists 'fellowship' as a hallmark of the early church (Acts 2:42), he had in mind not the Lord's Supper, but the collection, for the Greek word for fellowship (*koinōnia*) could also refer to the giving of money, and was used by Paul to describe his collection for the poor of Jerusalem. True fellowship always needs to find tangible expression.

Scriptures to reflect on

- 'They devoted themselves to the apostles' teaching and fellowship, to the breaking of bread and the prayers' (Acts 2:42).
- 'When you come together, each one has a hymn, a lesson, a revelation, a tongue, or an interpretation. Let all things be done for building up' (1 Corinthians 14:26).
- 'Be filled with the Spirit, as you sing psalms and hymns and spiritual songs among yourselves, singing and making melody to the Lord in your hearts' (Ephesians 5:18–19).
- 'I urge that supplications, prayers, intercessions, and thanksgivings should be made for everyone, for kings and all who are in high positions . . .' (1 Timothy 2:1–2).
- 'Give attention to the public reading of scripture' (1 Timothy 4:13).

43. Bring back the Bible!

Strange to say: the more 'Bible-believing' a Baptist church might claim to be, the less Scripture will have a place. Indeed, I will never forget one children's Sunday morning service led by members of a Scripture Union beach mission team that failed to include even one verse of Scripture! This children's service may have been an exception – or is it? I have the feeling that at many a so-called family service the reading of Scripture tends to be an unwelcome add-on. But family services apart, even in ordinary straightforward worship services, Scripture reading is often kept to a minimum. There are many Baptist churches which happily declare that the Bible is their guide in all matters of faith and practice, but have only one Scripture reading a service. And, what's more, in my experience that Scripture reading may often be only a few verses in length. In comparison with the more liturgical churches, our churches are starved of Scripture.

By contrast, in your average Anglican church at a Sunday service there will normally be three readings – from the Old Testament, the Epistles and the Gospels. This does not include any psalms that may be sung, nor the Ten Commandments that might be read. It is no exaggeration to say that the normal Anglican service of worship is literally peppered with Scripture, whereas in the average Baptist church Scripture is marginalized. True, the average Baptist sermon may be considerably longer than the average Anglican sermon, but that does not mean that we Baptists therefore somehow make up for the lack of Scripture reading. We need to get our priorities right, remembering, as John Wesley put it, that 'Although there may be chaff in the pulpit, there is always good grain at the lectern.'

My own practice is to ensure that there are always two main Scripture readings in every service: one from the Old Testament, and one from the New. In addition, the 'call to worship' normally takes the form of some verses from one of the psalms; and before we come to sing a clutch of contemporary worship songs the worship leader will always read an appropriate passage, which links in to the theme of these songs. So, one way or another, we seek to lace our services with Scriptures of various kinds. Furthermore, I believe that if we are to live up to our calling, then we Baptists must root our life together in Scripture, and I encourage people to bring their own Bibles to church. Because some people are put off by the present variety of versions, we have standardized Bible-reading by using just one version of Scripture. Although I personally prefer the New Revised Standard Bible (it is the most accurate English version and therefore the preferred English-language text of university theological faculties), we have opted for the Good News Bible on the ground that it is the most accessible of modern versions. We want to be a 'Bible-using' and 'Bible-friendly' church![1]

Faith comes by hearing
'Faith comes by Hearing' is the name of an innovative Bible Society project to encourage people to listen to the whole of the New Testament within a 40-day period (28 minutes a day!) and in this way restore the Bible to its central place in our individual lives. At first sight 'Faith comes by Hearing' appears to be a very modern approach to Scripture. Actually, it has been the traditional way of people learning about God. For the first fifteen hundred years or so of the church's existence faith only came 'by hearing' (see Romans 10:17). It was only five hundred years ago that mechanical printing was invented and that as a result it became possible for ordinary people to have our own private Bibles that we could read. Prior to

Gutenberg and the Luther Bible, the only way ordinary people heard the Word of God was to hear it read for them in church.

Paul, for instance, instructed Timothy to devote himself to 'the public reading of scripture' (1 Timothy 4:13). This practice of the public reading of Scripture had its roots in Judaism (see Nehemiah 8:8) and was continued in the synagogue. When Jesus was in the synagogue at Nazareth he was invited to read the Scriptures and then to comment on them. Timothy would have done the same. And so the tradition carried on. In the middle of the second century Justin Martyr wrote: 'On the day called Sunday, all who live in cities or in the country gather together to one place, and the memoirs of the apostles and the writings of the prophets are read, as long as time permits; then, when the reader has finished, the president speaks, instructing and exhorting the people to imitate these good things.'[2]

Today some might argue that the public reading of Scripture is less important because people have their own Bibles. But sadly, even Christian people do not necessarily read their Bibles. According to the Bible Society, 15% of regular churchgoers have never read anything from the Bible, and a further 17% of regular churchgoers have read nothing from the Bible in the last twelve months. As a result, one wit said that 'the best place to store your money is in a Bible, because it is unlikely to be opened'!

This is a serious situation, because a biblically illiterate church is a church that is confused both intellectually and morally, and which in turn lacks the motivation and the ability to live out and speak out the Christian faith. If people will not read the Bible for themselves, then we need to ensure that it is read, and read well, in church.

As Paul made clear to Timothy (2 Timothy 3:14–17), Scripture has a vital role to play, and in four respects in particular.

First, it leads us to Christ and to salvation. It speaks of a God who loves the world he has made and who sent his Son to be its Saviour.

Secondly, it teaches truth and corrects error about God, and about what he has done for us in Jesus. In Timothy's day there were people around who had some awfully warped views about God. Sadly, the same is true in our day too. All the more need for us to understand the basic doctrines of the Christian faith.

Thirdly, it shows us right and wrong behaviour. We are not simply called to love God and do what we like. God has a pattern for our living, and that pattern is to be found in Scripture. The Bible may not be a rule book, but it does contain very clear principles. Sadly, there are those who fail to take these principles seriously. In the words of the advertisement for a small-town Texan newspaper: 'Read your Bible to know what people ought to do. Read this paper to know what they actually do'!

Fourthly, it equips us for Christian service. Or as Peterson put it: 'through the Word we are put together and shaped up for the tasks God has for us' (2 Timothy 3:17, *The Message*). How can we, for instance, witness to Christ if we do not understand the faith, if we are unable to live out the faith?

Scriptures to reflect on

- 'Your word is a lamp to my feet / and a light to my path' (Psalm 119:105).
- 'But these are written so that you may believe that Jesus is the Messiah, the Son of God, and that through believing you may have life in his name' (John 20:31).
- 'They welcomed the message very eagerly and examined the scriptures every day' (Acts 17:11).
- 'The word of God is living and active, sharper than any two-edged sword . . .' (Hebrews 4:12).
- 'You will do well to be attentive . . . men and women moved by the Holy Spirit spoke from God' (2 Peter 1:19–21).

44. Be child-friendly!

Nothing gave me more pleasure recently than to see lots of children having fun at an evening service. True, it was an evening service with a difference. The service 'proper' lasted only 35 minutes, and even then it included a video of Eeyore's birthday party (it acted as a lead into my 8-minute address on God's party, to which we are all invited). The service was then followed by an ice-breaker question-naire, a game of Chinese laundry and then musical mats, followed by a veritable feast laid on by our African members – all in honour of my sixtieth birthday.

That evening the children discovered that church is a great place to be – a place where the family of God can come together and enjoy life together.

Years ago I remember one of my lady deacons telling me that it was more important for children to experience God's love through the love of his people than for them to learn of God's love from Sunday school lessons. At the time I was taken aback by this statement, but on reflection realized how right she was.

Our church, like many other Baptist churches, runs all kinds of activities for children, but activity itself is not enough. What is required is for children to see and experience love in action. Apart from love and laughter, what else can a church do to ensure that it is a place where children like to be?

One splendid idea, on which we stumbled by accident, is to allow children to play with computers with access to the Internet. The original intention of our cyber café was to be a low-key midweek evangelistic tool for attracting both younger and older people to our church. However, what we have discovered is that on a Sunday the cyber café is the place young children immediately head for. While their parents are busily engaged in setting up for Sunday school or whatever, the children have a whale of a time roaming the Net (naturally, the computers have been set up in such a way that unhelpful Web sites cannot be accessed). They are also learning that church need not be divorced from the world of today.

But what about the services themselves? They too need to be child-friendly. The first 20 or so minutes before the children go to their own teaching sessions we bear in mind the needs of the children. This does not mean that there has to be a 'children's talk' – in our church they tend to be a rarity. It does mean that prayers need to be simple enough to be understood by a 6-year-old; that Scripture readings are taken from the Good News Bible rather than the more difficult New International Version or New Revised Standard Version; and that hymns and songs should be able to have meaning for children. It doesn't, however, mean that everything therefore has to become childish – it simply means that the needs of our youngest worshippers are kept in mind.[1]

Children on the way

One Sunday morning a 6-year-old girl came up to me and asked to be baptized. As gently as possible, I told her she was too young, but that I looked forward to the day when I could and would baptize her.

My reason for declining her request was not that I questioned her sincerity. She truly loves the Lord Jesus and in her own childlike way has put her trust in him. However, unlike my friends from other Christian traditions (and indeed unlike many Southern Baptists in the USA) I felt I could not baptize her. For baptism is surely more than telling the world that we love Jesus? Among other things, baptism is the moment when we publicly die to self and resolve to live for Christ. Baptism presupposes that we have counted the cost and are willing to go the way of the cross. So in baptism we confess Jesus not just as our Saviour, but also as our Lord. Young children cannot make such a confession with any real depth of meaning – they have yet to learn what it means to bear the weight of the cross. It was for reasons such as these that I found myself having to say 'No' to the young girl at the door.

However, as the day wore on, I began to feel uneasy, not with my decision, but rather with the impact of the decision on the child in question. The last thing I wanted was for her to feel rejected. So, with the parents' permission, I went to visit the child and gave her a simple book about following Jesus, which over succeeding months she carefully went through with her mother.

One of my present goals is, with the help of others, to set up what in the early centuries of the Christian Church was known as a 'catechumenate'. Except that, while in the early church the 'catechumenate' was for adults preparing for baptism, this will be for young children. Indeed, I have already prepared a card with the following wording:

CENTRAL BAPTIST CHURCH, CHELMSFORD

CHILDREN ON THE WAY

'For God so loved the world that he gave his only Son,
so that everyone who believes in him may not die
but may have eternal life' (John 3:16).

We are delighted that you have accepted Jesus as your Saviour
and look forward to the day when you confess him
as Lord in baptism

Signed on behalf of the church
. . . . (Minister)
Date . . . .

Producing a card and getting it signed is, of course, not enough. The word 'catechumenate' comes from a Greek verb meaning to 'instruct'. Although we have an active Sunday School, additional 'instruction' and indeed encouragement will be necessary. How precisely we will do this I do not know, for clearly we are not running a normal baptismal class. Here is an area for further thought. Hopefully, here too is an area for learning from others. Are there churches practising believer's baptism that are already into running a 'catechumenate' for young children?

As any experienced pastor knows, the question of what we do with young children who want to be baptized has always been with us. However, in recent years the issue has become more pressing because in the Anglican church in particular there has been a move to encourage young children to take communion. What is more, this encouragement is present not just on a Sunday, but during the week. For, in many church schools children as part of their school-day religious education are taken to church and offered bread and wine. Inevitably, this raises questions in the minds of children from Baptist homes, questions that relate not simply to the Lord's Supper but also to baptism. All the more reason for 'baptistic' Christians to help their children along the way.

Scriptures to reflect on
- 'Unless you change and become like children, you will never enter the kingdom of heaven' (Matthew 18:3).
- 'If any of you put a stumbling-block before one of these little ones who believe in me, it would be better for you if a great millstone were fastened around your neck and you were drowned in the depth of the sea' (Matthew 18:6).
- 'Let the little children come to me' (Mark 10:14).
- 'From childhood you have known the sacred writings that are able to instruct you for salvation through faith in Christ Jesus' (2 Timothy 3:15).
- 'Grow in the grace and knowledge of our Lord and Saviour Jesus Christ' (2 Peter 3:18).

45. Preach for about 20 minutes

'Talk about God and talk about 20 minutes' used to be the rule of thumb for Baptist preachers. And a good rule it was too. I will never forget F. F. Bruce once wrily commenting to me: 'Preachers who've got nothing to say need 40 minutes, those with something to say need only 20 minutes.'

I know that in some churches 40 minutes is the norm, but I sometimes wonder to what extent the preachers of such sermons have truly prepared their sermon. In this respect a remark of Mark Twain comes to mind when he sent a long letter to a friend. He apologized for the length and said it would have been shorter, but he didn't have time. The fact is that longer does not mean better. Indeed, one Roman Catholic bishop advised his clergy that when they had finished preparing their usual-length sermon, they should cut it in half. It may involve minor rewriting, but he said: 'What's left is the very best material.'

Certainly, I think that if preachers were to go to the trouble of writing out their sermons in full (rather than simply use headings) they might well find that their sermons would be clearer, deeper and shorter. But when it comes to the length of the sermon, there are other factors at play.

There is, for instance, the attention span of the congregation – most people are not used to sitting still and listening to a 20-minute monologue. I confess that on more than one occasion I have fallen asleep when the preacher has gone on – and on!

Then, there is the issue of ensuring that there is balance in a service. For people do not simply come to church to listen to the preacher: there needs to be time for worship, prayer, reading the Scriptures, celebrating around the Table. My experience of other churches where longer sermons are the norm is that the prayers of intercession are squeezed out, and the reading of the Scriptures is truncated, while the Lord's Supper is often regarded as an addendum.

But there is yet another issue, which is not often recognized, and that concerns the children, who in most of our churches tend to go to their classes after the first 20 minutes or so of worship. The fact is that there is a limit as to how long untrained teachers (and many people working in our Sunday schools are understandably not professional teachers) can look after their charges. Here I have in mind the difficulties posed by the unruly or even disturbed child: 50 minutes is a long time to care for such a child. The danger is that the longer the service goes on, the more likely it is that one day the patience of one of the untrained teachers will snap, and then all the forces of child protection come into play. Preachers of long sermons are not being fair to their Sunday school staff. So let's ensure that 20 (or if need be 25) minutes remains the norm.[1]

Preaching has not had its day

Preaching (for Protestantism at least) lies at the heart of ministry. In North America the pastor is often known as 'the preacher'. Preaching for many ministers is their number one priority.

But all is not well with preaching. Many preachers are boring, long-winded and irrelevant. The question therefore arises: Has preaching had its day? Just as churches are rapidly scrapping their pews today, should they scrap their pulpits too?

Preaching, it is said, because it is non-cooperative communication, is no longer suitable for our time. It is like using a paraffin lamp in the age of electric light. The sermon has been described as 'a monstrous monologue by a moron to mutes'.[2] Furthermore, not only is preaching often boring; it is also frequently remarkably ineffective. American research has indicated that immediately following the worship service, fewer than one-third of the persons tested could give a reasonably clear statement of the primary 'question' of the sermon or the 'answer' suggested in the message. In another research project the results were even worse: 21% of the 271 persons (who all felt that the sermon was either 'superior' or 'good) could reflect the preacher's central message clearly and accurately. And, of course, none of this research indicated whether or not those who did remember what the sermon was about, actually changed their minds or behaviour as a result of what they heard!

In the light of such criticisms and comments, it is tempting to ditch preaching altogether. Haven't we preachers got better things to do with our time? Just think of all the hours put into sermon preparation week by week. Then multiply these hours by the number of sermons preached in the country. It is estimated that in England and Wales alone some 50,000 sermons are delivered each week. Think of all the positive things that could be done with the time devoted to preaching!

But, of course, it is not as simple as that. The abuse of the medium does not invalidate the medium. Let me illustrate. Many video and DVD shops do a flourishing trade in hiring out films glorifying violence and sex. But does the abuse of that medium necessarily invalidate that medium? Of course not! The same argument applies to preaching. The fact that much preaching falls far short of the mark does not necessarily mean that all preaching should therefore be scrapped. There are times when preaching can be remarkably effective. Many a Christian can testify to a time when, quite unexpectedly, God broke through and addressed them directly by means of a sermon. True, this is not an experience that happens to everybody every Sunday, but even that does not invalidate the ordinary preaching that goes on Sunday by Sunday.

All this is well illustrated in a correspondence that took place a number of years ago in the former *British Weekly*. It began with the publishing of this provocative letter:

Dear Sir,
It seems ministers feel their sermons are very important and spend a great deal of time preparing them. I have been attending church quite

regularly for 30 years and I have probably heard 3,000 of them. To my consternation, I discover I cannot remember a single sermon. I wonder if a minister's time might be more profitably spent on something else?

The *British Weekly* received a storm of responses. The correspondence was finally ended by the following letter:

Dear Sir,
I have been married for 30 years. During that time I have eaten 32,850 meals – mostly my wife's cooking. Suddenly I have discovered I cannot remember the menu of a single meal. And yet . . . I have the distinct impression that without them, I would have starved to death long ago.

Not all preaching has to be remembered to be effective. On the other hand, we must not be fooled into believing that there is no room for improvement. Far from it: there is much room for improvement. But this does not mean that the basic institution of preaching has had its day and is now ready to be scrapped. For if preaching has had its day, then what else would we put in its place? How else would the gospel be communicated?

Scriptures to reflect on
- 'Jesus came to Galilee, proclaiming the good news of God' (Mark 1:14).
- 'We . . . will devote ourselves to prayer and to serving the word' (Acts 6:4).
- 'All of us are here in the presence of God to listen to all that the Lord has commanded you to say' (Acts 10:33).
- 'I am not ashamed of the gospel; it is the power of God for salvation to everyone who has faith' (Romans 1:16).
- 'We proclaim Christ crucified' (1 Corinthians 1:23).

46. Make good use of the Sunday after Christmas

By Christmas lunchtime most pastors will have had their surfeit of services. The Sunday before Christmas will have been dominated by carol services, then comes Christmas Eve, then Christmas Day. It's an exhausting business. And then, before you can breathe, another Sunday comes. To make matters worse, this year 'Boxing Day' is a Sunday. It really is tough – everybody else is able to relax over Christmas, but not the poor pastor, who has to spend the two festival days working. And before you can say 'Jack Robinson', there are uplifting sermons to be prepared to mark the New Year. True, most, if not all, church organizations observe the Christmas break, but death is no respecter of Christmas – one Christmas I had six deaths taking place in the fellowship over the Christmas period!

So what can be done to make the pastoral load easier? First of all, cancel the evening service on the Sunday after Christmas – the only people who would turn out would be a few guilt-ridden church members. Some might say cancel the morning service too, for certainly this year many of us will be going to church three days running. And yet I would be loathe to do that – surely Sunday worship has to have the primacy, even at Christmas. An alternative (for the pastor, though not for the people) is to take off that Sunday and get somebody else to preach that day.

My preferred solution, however, is to use the Sunday to thank God, or rather to get the church to thank God. Yes, get the church to thank God for the year that is past. Turn the service into an occasion for short (5 minutes maximum!) testimonies to the goodness of God. One person might speak of the joy of coming to know the Lord through an Alpha course; another of God's encouragement while away at university; a third, perhaps, of her gratitude to God for the gift of a child; while another might speak of the strength received to cope with bereavement. There are all kinds of reasons why people might thank God: a new job, a new home, a new church family; a silver wedding or a golden wedding; healing of relationships or healing of body. There is much to be said for each testimony being linked with a verse of Scripture. For inevitably testimonies are subjective, whereas there is a certain objectiveness about the Word of God.

Clearly, such a service demands some preparation – people need to be asked to speak, even if one opens the service to others to share an informal word of testimony. However, from the perspective of the pastor, the great thing is that if there are five or six testimonies, there is no need for a full-blooded sermon – a 5-minute address at the most is sufficient. And as for the congregation, they won't feel short-changed that day, but rather they will be uplifted as they listen to others tell of God's gracious action in their lives. What technically is a 'Low Sunday' in the church's liturgical year becomes a 'High Sunday'.[1]

Thank God for the year that is past

Although the last Sunday of the year falls within the twelve days of Christmas, for many it is a relief to begin a service with a hymn like 'Now thank we all our God' rather than yet another carol. Similarly, it comes as a welcome change for the opening prayer to focus on the year that is past, rather than on the Babe of Bethlehem; for example:

> Father God, on this last Sunday of the year, as we look back we have so much for which to thank you. Thank you for all the good times: for all the happiness and joy that has been ours, for every evidence of your love and goodness. Thank you too that even in the hard times you were

there: you gave us new strength; you helped us not only to cope, but also to grow. Yes, Lord, each one of us can look back and be thankful. But, we are also sad. For in spite of the pattern given to us by your Son, the Lord Jesus, we have been slow to learn of him and reluctant to bear his cross; we confess that we have failed you and failed one another. But how we thank you that you are more than willing to forgive us and allow us to have a new start. So forgive us, and fit us by your grace for whatever lies before us in the days to come.

For those not bound by the readings of the day, a psalm like Psalm 103 is very fitting, followed perhaps by some simple worship songs praising God for his goodness.

Then the testimonies, interspersed with appropriate songs. Last year the testimonies in our church were hung around the theme of 'new': a newly baptized person thanked God for the past year, then a new member, a newly married woman, a new parent, a new grandparent, a new deacon, a new student, a person with a new job, and another who had engaged in a new venture. Each of these testimonies had to be concise (3 minutes maximum), for we then opened up the service to anybody to come and say in one sentence why they were grateful to God for the year that was past.

The testimonies were followed by a reading from Revelation 21:1–5, and a brief exposition of God's promise 'See, I am making all things new'.

The service closed with the singing of the great Welsh hymn 'Guide me, O Thou great Jehovah', and the blessing incorporating words from Minnie Haskins, made famous by King George V in a radio broadcast:

I said to the man who stood at the Gate of the Year, 'Give me a light that I may tread safely into the unknown.' And he replied, 'Go out into the darkness and put your hand into the hand of God. That shall be to you better than light and safer than a known way.' May that Almighty hand guide and uphold us all; through Jesus Christ our Lord.

Scriptures to reflect on

- 'I trust in you, O LORD; / I say: "You are my God." / My times are in your hand . . .' (Psalm 31:14–15).

- 'I will sing of your steadfast love, O LORD, for ever; / with my mouth I will proclaim your faithfulness to all generations' (Psalm 89:1).
- 'Forgetting what lies behind and straining forward to what lies ahead, I press on towards the goal for the prize of the heavenly call of God in Christ Jesus' (Philippians 3:13–14).
- 'Jesus Christ is the same yesterday and today and for ever' (Hebrews 13:8).
- 'Now to him who is able to keep you from falling, and to make you stand without blemish in the presence of his glory with rejoicing, to the only God our Saviour, through Jesus Christ our Lord, be glory, majesty, power, and authority, before all time and now and for ever' (Jude 24).

47. Celebrate Easter

'If there's no resurrection for Christ,' wrote the apostle Paul, 'everything we've told you is smoke and mirrors, and everything you've staked your life on is smoke and mirrors . . . And if Christ wasn't raised, then all you're doing is wandering about in the dark, as lost as ever . . . If all we get out of Christ is a little inspiration for a few short years, we're a pretty sorry lot' (1 Corinthians 15:16–18, *The Message*).

Yet, we have to admit that from a purely rational perspective belief in the resurrection of Jesus is absurd. Dead people do not rise from the dead. Death is always final. Or is it? Lord Byron claimed that there are times when 'truth is . . . stranger than fiction'.

Faith in the resurrection has nothing to do with blind belief. Christian faith does not involve shutting one's eyes and with the White Queen in Alice believing six impossible things before breakfast. The great eighteenth-century German philosopher Immanuel Kant was wrong when he stated: 'I must put aside knowledge to make room for faith.' Faith does not displace knowledge. The two can go hand in hand. Christian faith always involves reasonable believing – and this is true even if reason has its limits.

There is never a stage when we need to put aside knowledge to make room for faith – and this is true not least of faith in the resurrection. When it comes to the resurrection of Jesus, there is evidence to be weighed, facts to be considered.

Tom Wright, Bishop of Durham, after weighing up all the evidence in his massive tome *The Resurrection of the Son of God* writes: 'I conclude that the historian, of whatever persuasion, has no option but to affirm both the empty tomb and the "meetings" with Jesus as "historical events" ... they took place as real events; they were significant events; they are, in the normal sense required by historians, provable events; historians can and should write about them. We cannot account for early Christianity without them.'[1]

A very different book on the resurrection was written by Pinchas Lapide, a German-Jewish rabbi who, although not a Christian, argued for the resurrection as a historical event. He wrote: 'I cannot rid myself of the impression that some modern Christian theologians are ashamed of the material facticity of the resurrection ... For all these Christians who believe in the incarnation (something which I am unable to do) but have difficulty with the historically understood resurrection of Jesus, the word of Jesus of the "blind guides, straining out a gnat and swallowing a camel" (Matthew 23:24) probably applies.'[2]

Yes, the evidence for the resurrection of Jesus is overwhelming. In the words of Lord Darling, a former Lord Chief Justice of England:

> We, as Christians, are asked to take a very great deal on trust: the teachings, for example, and the miracles of Jesus. If we had to take all on trust, I, for one, should be skeptical. The crux of the problem of whether Jesus was or was not what he proclaimed himself to be, must surely depend on the truth or otherwise of the resurrection. On that greatest point we are not merely asked to have faith. In its favour as a living truth there exists such overwhelming evidence, positive and negative, factual and circumstantial, that no intelligent jury in the world could fail to bring in the verdict that the resurrection story is true.[3]

Christ is risen. Hallelujah!

Easter prayers

A prayer of praise

'Lord Jesus, we praise you, for you have risen from the dead! We praise you that by your cross you have defeated the power of the Evil

One and through your resurrection we are now set free. Lord, without your resurrection our faith would be empty, and we would be without hope. But you are alive, and we rejoice and wonder in the mystery of your presence among us.'

A prayer for our church
'Lord Jesus, on this day of new life and freedom, we pray for our church. Lord, may our life together be characterized by new life and freedom. To this end, free us from the shackles of crippling guilt and life-denying legalism. Through our lives as through our words help us to proclaim the good news of healing, forgiveness and hope.'

A prayer for those experiencing darkness
'Lord Jesus, your friends and disciples must have been utterly bereft at your death, with all their hope and purpose broken. so we pray now for those who are in darkness and pain today: those facing the keen disappointment of broken hopes; lives damaged by broken relationships and trust; people with broken hearts; bodies broken by torture and spirits broken by injustice. Lord, in the darkness bring light.'

A prayer for those who are dying
'Lord Jesus, on this day of life and resurrection we pray for those who are even now going through the valley of the shadow of death. Surround them with your presence and peace. Give strength and comfort too to families and their friends as they see their loved one leave them on their final journey.'

A prayer for ourselves
'Lord Jesus, as we celebrate your triumph over death and the grave, may we also make it the model for our living. Help us to identify in our lives all that should rightly die – redundant relationships, tired habits and fruitless longings. And by the power with which your Father raised you from the grave, resurrect in our lives faith, hope and love.'

Scriptures to reflect on
- 'They left the tomb quickly with fear and great joy' (Matthew 28:8).

- 'Why do you look for the living among the dead? He is not here, but has risen' (Luke 24:5).
- 'Thomas answered him, "My Lord and my God!"' (John 20:28).
- 'This Jesus God raised up, and of that all of us are witnesses' (Acts 2:32).
- 'We know that the one who raised the Lord Jesus will raise us also with Jesus' (2 Corinthians 4:14).

48. Celebrate Harvest

There used to be three occasions in the year when people got sentimental and were inclined to go to church – Christmas, Easter and Harvest. Christmas (and to a lesser degree Easter) are still a great draw. I confess that I am not so sure how much of an attraction Harvest is today to the general public. Is this in part because most churches have given up on decorating their churches? I believe there is something to be said for a token display. Or has Harvest ceased to be a draw because an ever-increasing number of us are losing touch with the countryside. Let's be honest, it doesn't make much sense for 'townies' to sing 'We plough the fields and scatter' when the only time they have seen a plough is in a museum. Most of us have become so distant from the countryside that we can't distinguish wheat from barley, or rye from oats. And yet the hymn does enable us to express our gratitude to God and acknowledge our dependence upon him.

Yes, it must be right to celebrate Harvest. True, it is not a Christian festival, in the sense that unlike Christmas and Easter it is not rooted in the life of Jesus. And yet, we Christians surely have a doctrine of creation as well as a doctrine of redemption, do we not? So let's major on Harvest and encourage people to be grateful to God for meeting their physical needs.

But Harvest is more than an occasion for encouraging thankfulness. Harvest is also an occasion for arousing people's consciences to the needs of the developing world. It's a time to talk about our nation's meanness and selfishness towards the poor. Don't be afraid to be forthright. By and large the prophets weren't lynched; they were only thoroughly disliked. Most churches these days have understandably given up on encouraging people to bring garden produce to church – what does one do with over-ripe plums, or indeed what do the elderly or the sick do with over-ripe plums? Instead, most churches encourage their members to give to a developing-world project sponsored by Operation Agri or the BMS. I like to suggest to people that they consider giving to the developing-world project the amount of money they spent that week at the supermarket. Indeed, a good visual would be to borrow a large supermarket shopping trolley, fill it with goods a typical family would buy, and then at the Harvest Sunday morning service take out the goods, one by one, and tot up the cost involved. Then multiply the cost by the number of families in the church, and say that's the minimum amount you expect from the church that day – but do it with love and humour!

Harvest, however, is more than an opportunity to raise money. It also provides a wonderful evangelistic opportunity. This is the day to preach a sermon on the rich fool, on the Lord who will sort out the wheat from the weeds, the Lord who is the bread of life. This year, for instance, I have set myself the task of preaching on the grain of wheat, which if it 'dies' produces many grains (John 12:24).

So, let's make the most of this day. Let's challenge our people to use nicely printed harvest leaflets and invite their neighbours. I guarantee that many will accept a personal invitation, if given.[1]

A Harvest Supper with a difference
'On Sunday ... the harvest "bring and share" supper has become a harvest "pudding party"! The "party" (there will be a few games!) begins at 5.30 pm and will lead into a family-friendly service featuring the needs of the Hill Tribe people of Thailand. Everybody is asked to bring a pudding – ideally a pudding with an overseas flavour: e.g. Tiramisu from Italy, or a Kiwi Surprise from New Zealand, or Baklava from Turkey, or lychees from China. There will be a prize

for the most scrumptious puddings – the ministers will be the judges! Drinks will be provided. Along with the puddings, please also bring a generous gift (the equivalent of your weekly supermarket shop?) to go towards this year's project.'

Scriptures to reflect on

- 'As long as the earth endures, / seedtime and harvest, cold and heat, / summer and winter, day and night, / shall not cease' (Genesis 8:22).
- 'You visit the earth and water it, / you greatly enrich it ... / You crown the year with your bounty ...' (Psalm 65:9, 11).
- 'Life does not consist in the abundance of possessions' (see the parable of the rich fool, Luke 12:15).
- 'The living God ... has not left himself without a witness in doing good – giving you rains from heaven and fruitful seasons, and filling you with food and your hearts with joy' (Acts 14:15, 17).
- 'Christ has been raised from the dead, the first fruits of those who have died' (1 Corinthians 15:20).

49. Preach about money

Preaching about money is not something I like to do. In part, this is because I know that I have to practise what I preach! And in part too because I know that there are always some people in the congregation who take exception the moment they hear a preacher mention money. And yet, I feel I would be doing less than my duty if I omitted to teach on one of the basics of the Christian life. So normally once a year in the spring I preach about money.

In the first place, I believe that there is need for clear teaching about the principles of giving. In particular, I believe that we need to teach our young people that it is never too early to give. When for instance I became a church member in my early teens, I was given a set of offering envelopes in which I religiously put my sixpence. It didn't make much difference to the total offering, but it did instil into me the discipline of giving. As the American Baptist, John Rockefeller, once said: 'If I hadn't learnt to tithe my first dollar, I would never have tithed my first million.' Yes, however high or low our income may be, all of us have a duty to give.

I also believe that there are times when we need to challenge the people of God to give more. Certainly, having just gone through a £2 million redevelopment scheme, we have found it necessary on a number of occasions to present a financial challenge. Some 'superspiritual' members objected and said that we should simply trust God to supply our needs. They piously cited George Müller who made it a principle never to mention the financial needs of his orphanages. Instead, he simply 'prayed the money in'.

I don't buy that argument. The fact is that God normally supplies our needs through people, and in order for God to do that, people need to know what the needs are. I find it significant that the apostle Paul never prayed money in. Rather, he believed in appealing for money. In 2 Corinthians, for example, he devoted two whole chapters to the subject. In other letters, he comes back to the subject of money time and again. Jesus too was never embarrassed (see, for instance, Matthew 6:19–21, 24). I am told that one out of every six verses in the Gospels has to do with the right and wrong use of material possessions; and that sixteen out of thirty-eight parables have to do with the right and wrong use of material possessions.

I find it interesting that on one occasion Jesus sat in front of the temple collection box and watched people putting in their offering (Mark 12:41); as far as Jesus was concerned, giving was not a private manner! Nor indeed does the story of Ananias and Sapphira (Acts 5:1–11) encourage secrecy in giving. Why is it then that for some church people money has become the great unmentionable? I wonder, does their unease reflect shortcomings in their personal discipleship?[1]

How should we give?
The apostle Paul envisaged that Christians should put aside money on a weekly basis, but that was at a time when people were normally paid daily or sometimes weekly. Today, many of us are paid monthly, and so as far as I am concerned it makes sense for me to give monthly.

Many people give by monthly standing order, and understandably so. If we pay our utility bills by standing order, then why not pay our dues to God this way? It certainly makes life easier for the treasurer. In this so-called cashless society, many have little cash in their pocket; instead, their wallets or purses bulge with cards. True, they could write a cheque, but the advantage of a standing order is that people don't forget their dues. However, there is an even more efficient way of giving to the church: gift-aiding. This surely is the only responsible way for Christian tax-payers to give to the church.

The one apparent drawback to giving as you earn or to giving by standing order is that when the offering bags come round, we have no money to put into the bags. But so what? There is no sense in giving by standing order and then putting a pound coin, for instance, in the bag just for the sake of appearances. Indeed, because of the advantages of gift-aiding and the like, any casual giving of that nature makes no sense. Far better to let the bags go by.

To reflect the changed patterns of giving, in our church the offering is no longer a separate act in the service; rather, we take up the offering in the singing of a song of praise. Furthermore, in the offertory prayer we make clear that we are presenting not simply the gifts but ourselves; and that we are not just dedicating the money we have given to God (by whatever means) but also the week that lies ahead.

As a result of people becoming more businesslike in their giving, in our church at least, only a minority of people use the offering bags on a Sunday evening. At one stage we experimented with a 'Give-As-You-Enter' scheme, whereby a receptacle was placed at the door for gifts. The gifts were then brought forward at an appointed moment in the service – but without the need for stewards to 'work the aisles'. At the time it seemed a good idea, but in fact we discovered that we were considerably worse off, because most people ignored the collecting box!

Scriptures to reflect on
- 'They [the Macedonian Christians] gave themselves first to the Lord' (2 Corinthians 8:5).
- 'The one who sows sparingly will also reap sparingly, and the one who sows bountifully will also reap bountifully' (2 Corinthians 9:6).
- 'Each of you must give as you have made up your mind, not reluctantly or under compulsion, for God loves a cheerful giver' (2 Corinthians 9:7).
- 'God is able to provide you with every blessing in abundance, so that by always having enough of everything, you may share abundantly in every good work' (2 Corinthians 9:8).
- 'Thanks be to God for his indescribable gift!' (2 Corinthians 9:15).

50. Teach tithing

It's an interesting fact that the prophets did not teach the importance of giving. They assumed it. As far as they were concerned, it was an integral part of everyday religion to give at least a 'tithe' (one tenth) of all one's income to God. What was true of them, was also true of Jesus. Nowhere in the Gospels does he command his disciples to tithe – but appears to assume that they will. Indeed, the only thing for which Jesus ever commended the scribes and Pharisees of his day was their tithing (see Matthew 23:23).

When we move from the Gospels to Paul's letters, we find no reference to tithing as such, but we do find that Paul devotes quite a bit of space to the subject of giving (see 2 Corinthians 8 – 9). It is clear that Paul was a believer in 'proportionate' giving (see 1 Corinthians 16:2), which actually comes very close to the idea of tithing.

Some people today argue that tithing is a form of legalism, foreign to the spirit of the Gospel; they say: 'We are no longer under law, but under grace' (Romans 6:14). That is true, but it is no reason for those of us who live under the new covenant of grace to give less than those who only knew the old covenant. Indeed, if anything, it is an argument for us today to give more.

I find it significant that when Paul writes about giving to the

Corinthians, he doesn't major on the duties and responsibilities of Christian giving; rather, he speaks about the 'privilege' (2 Corinthians 8:4) of giving to God's work. For him giving was essentially an indication of one's love for the Lord (see 2 Corinthians 8:8–9). Paul, I'm sure, would have been amazed to have discovered that some people deduce that giving out of love rather than giving out of duty results in less than giving a tenth. Surely, the reverse should be true. Indeed, the more we understand what God has done for us in Jesus, the more we want to give to God. Unfortunately, those who argue against tithing as a form of legalism give the impression that they want to give to God as little as they can, rather than as much as they can.

So I myself tithe – and encourage (as distinct from pressurize) my church members to consider tithing. Indeed, because of the challenge of a major building project, many of us have double-tithed for a number of years, and at least one couple has triple-tithed. In so doing we have discovered great blessing, both in the life of our church as also in our individual lives. For, as the prophet Malachi knew, when we give out of love, then the Lord in his love gives in return (Malachi 3:10). We have discovered that although we may not have all the money we might want, we do have all the money we need. What's more, we have discovered the happiness that money can never buy – the deep satisfaction and joy of having a share in God's work.

Although I doubt whether Winston Churchill ever practised tithing, he hit upon some truth when he said: 'We make a living by what we get, but we make a life by what we give.' Or as Jesus said: 'There is more happiness in giving than in receiving' (Acts 20:35). So let me encourage you, dear reader, to tithe, and, where appropriate, to discover too the difference that gift-aiding from source (Give As You Earn) makes![1]

Overcome 'cirrhosis of the giver'

According to Tom Saunders, a churchwarden in Gabalfa, South Wales:

> 'Cirrhosis of the giver' was discovered early in the life of the church by Ananias and Sapphira (Acts 5). It is an acute condition which renders the patient's hand immovable when he is called upon to raise it in the

direction of the wallet or purse and then to the offering plate. The remedy is to remove the patient from the house of God, since it is clinically observable that this condition does not occur in other places such as the supermarket, restaurants or clubs. Of course, the best therapy, a sure and lasting cure, is to get right with God, as this is a condition symptomatic of a more serious problem: heart-trouble.[2]

This complaint is not new. Malachi accused his contemporaries of cheating God by failing to give to him their 'tithes and offerings' (Malachi 3:8).

In the Old Testament the Israelites were required to give a tenth of everything to God – not just their money, but their crops, flocks and herds. The tithe was not to consist of the dregs, but of the best of people's possessions (Leviticus 27:30–32). It is unfortunate that we speak of Oxfam shops as 'charity' shops – for it equates charity with giving away things we don't want, whereas true Christian charity only gives the best!

Malachi believed that giving should go beyond the tithe and should include 'offerings' (Malachi 3:8) too. Tithing is what God expects of us; offerings are gifts that go beyond the norm. Strictly speaking, we 'pay' our tithes and 'give' our offerings. Many believe that if they give the full whack of 10%, then they have really arrived when it comes to giving – whereas in fact they have only just begun to give.

This challenge to give is also found in the New Testament. Paul, for instance, pricked the self-satisfied consciences of the Christians at Corinth by pointing to the example of the Macedonian churches: 'they were extremely generous in their giving, even though they were very poor' (2 Corinthians 8:2, Good News Bible). Many would think that poverty would be a fair reason for not giving: 'I'm on benefit ... I'm on a student grant ... I've got a wife and six kids to support.' But the heart truly in love with the Lord Jesus always finds ways to give, even in poverty. The Macedonians gave 'beyond their means' (8:3). They brought not only their tithes to the Lord, but also their offerings.

Paul in tackling 'cirrhosis of the giver' also adopted another tack. Like Malachi (see Malachi 3:10) he emphasized the benefits of giving. God is nobody's debtor. 'God is able to provide you with every blessing in abundance' (9:8). God multiplies our resources (9:10), so we can never outgive him!

God doesn't promise to give us all the luxuries this world affords, but he does promise to meet our needs. And although the benefits are not always in cash, we are never the losers with God. As Ebenezer Scrooge discovered, a closed-fist philosophy brings little blessing, if any.

Simon Webley talks of the six genuine surprises that come to a person who begins to tithe:

> He will be surprised at the amount of money he has for the Lord's work, at the deepening of his spiritual life in paying the tithe, at his ease in meeting his own obligations with the nine-tenths, at the ease with which he is able to go on from one-tenth to larger giving, at the increased sense of stewardship over the nine-tenths that remain, and at himself for not adopting the plan sooner![3]

Scriptures to reflect on

- 'Bring the full tithe ... and thus put me to the test, says the LORD of hosts; see if I will not open the windows of heaven for you and pour down for you an overflowing blessing' (Malachi 3:10).
- 'Store up for yourselves treasures in heaven ... For where your treasure is, there your heart will be also' (Matthew 6:20–21).
- 'Give, and it will be given to you ... the measure you give will be the measure you get back' (Luke 6:38).
- 'On the first day of the week, each of you is to put aside and save whatever extra you earn' (1 Corinthians 16:2; Good News Bible: 'money, in proportion to what you have earned').
- 'You know the generous act of our Lord Jesus Christ, that though he was rich, yet for your sakes he became poor, so that by his poverty you might become rich' (2 Corinthians 8:9).

Notes

Introduction

1 Once the 'supplement' was a later article.

Chapter 1

1 John W. Doberstein, *The Minister's Prayer Book* (London: Collins, 1986).
2 *Celebrating Common Prayer: A Version of the Daily Office SSF* (London: Mowbray, 1992).
3 Don Carson, *For the Love of God* (Leicester: IVP, 1998).
4 'The minister's devotional life', *Baptist Times*, 25 March 2004.

Chapter 2

1 'Pressurised to grow?', *Baptist Times*, 11 March 2004.
2 Gordon Bridger, *The Man from Outside* (Leicester: IVP, 1978), 208.
3 D. Tidball, *Builders and Fools* (Leicester: IVP, 1999), 9.
4 Ibid., 15.

Chapter 3

1 'How hard do ministers work?', *Baptist Times*, 18 March 2004.

Chapter 4

1 'Ministers need appraisals', *Baptist Times*, 22 April 2004.
2 Quoted by Jill M. Hudson, *Evaluating Ministry: Principles and Processes for Clergy and Congregation* (Bethesda: Alban Institute, 1992), 7.

Chapter 5

1 'Retreats maintain integrity', *Baptist Times*, 11 December 2003.

2 William L. Lane, *Hebrews 9 – 13*, Word Biblical Commentary (Dallas: Word, 1991), 410.

3 Derek Tidball, *Builders and Fools* (Leicester: IVP, 1999), 148.

4 Quote from John Perry, *Christian Leadership* (London: Hodder & Stoughton, 1983), 15.

Chapter 6

1 Paul Beasley-Murray and Alan Wilkinson, *Turning the Tide* (London: Bible Society, 1980), 34.

2 Lynn Anderson, 'Why I've Stayed', *Leadership* 7.3 (1986), 77.

3 'How long should a minister stay on in one church?', *Baptist Times*, 6 May 2004.

4 Roy M. Oswald, Gail D. Hinand, William Chris Hobood and Barton M. Lloyd, *New Visions for the Long Pastorate* (Washington, DC: Alban, 1983), 30.

5 Ibid., 87.

6 Eugene Peterson, *Under the Unpredictable Plant: An Exploration in Vocational Holiness* (Grand Rapids: Eerdmans; Leominster: Gracewing, 1992), 21.

Chapter 7

1 'When should a minister move on?', *Baptist Times*, 1 July 2004.

2 David Cormack, *Managing Change* (Bromley: MARC, no date), 71.

Chapter 8

1 'Churchgoing is not enough', *Baptist Times*, 13 November 2003.

2 John Mallison, *Building Small Groups in the Christian Community* (London: Scripture Union, 1978).

Chapter 9

1 (London: Fontana, 1975), 50–62.

2 'Real churches need small groups', *Baptist Times*, 10 February 2005.

Chapter 10

1 'Dissent in the church meeting', *Baptist Times*, 9 December 2004.

Chapter 11

1 'How do we handle church discipline?', *Baptist Times*, 29 April 2004.

2 See Alastair Campbell, 'The authority of fraternal admonition', *Fraternal* 208 (July 1984), 12–16.

3 Martin Luther, *A Commentary on St Paul's Epistle to the Galatians* (English Translation; London: James Clarke, 1953), 538.

Chapter 12

1 Lyle E. Schaller, *21 Bridges to the 21st Century* (Nashville: Abingdon, 1994), 24.

2 'Church rolls need to be revised on a regular basis', *Baptist Times*, 3 June 2004.

Chapter 13

1 'Livening up the AGM', *Baptist Times*, 5 August 2004.

Chapter 14

1 'Basic pastoral care', *Baptist Times*, 4 December 2003.

Chapter 15

1 'Bringing God into life's special occasions', *Baptist Times*, 20 September 2004.

Chapter 16

1 'Is cohabitation wrong?', *Baptist Times*, 22 July 2004.

Chapter 17

1 'Should divorcees remarry in church?, *Baptist Times*, 29 July 2004.

Chapter 18

1 'What should we do with painful memories?', *Baptist Times*, 11 November 2004.

Chapter 19

1 Kennon L. Callahan, *Twelve Keys to an Effective Church* (San Francisco: Harper, 1983), 12.

2 'The day of pastoral visiting is not over', *Baptist Times*, 17 March 2005.

Chapter 20

1 'Healing in the church', *Baptist Times*, 24 June 2004.

Chapter 21

1 'Old people need Jesus too!', *Baptist Times*, 7 April 2005.

Chapter 22

1 'Helping the terminally ill', *Baptist Times*, 12 February 2004.
2 M. Scott Peck, *Further Along the Road Less Travelled* (New York: Simon & Schuster, 1994), 49.
3 Bill Kirkpatrick, *Going Forth* (London: Darton, Longman & Todd, 1997), 10.
4 Ibid., 83.

Chapter 23

1 S. Pearce Carey, *William Carey* (London: Carey, 1942), 120.
2 'Tributes at a funeral', *Baptist Times*, 20 January 2005.

Chapter 24

1 'No short cuts when grieving', *Baptist Times*, 5 February 2004.

Chapter 25

1 Graham Tomlin, *The Provocative Church* (London: SPCK, 2002), 10.
2 'Jesus is sick of words', *Baptist Times*, 29 January 2004.

Chapter 26

1 William Easum, *Dancing with Dinosaurs: Ministry in a Hostile and Hurting World* (Nashville: Abingdon, 1993).
2 'Evangelism is a necessity', *Baptist Times*, 15 January 2004.

Chapter 27

1 C. Peter Wagner, *Your Church Can Grow* (Glendale: Regal, 1976), 110.
2 Robin Gill, *A Vision for Growth* (London: SPCK, 1994), 3.
3 'Church growth is desirable', *Baptist Times*, 22 January 2004.
4 See C. Peter Wagner, *Leading your Church to Growth* (Ventura, CA: Regal, 1984), 41–72.
5 Peter Drucker, *Management* (New York: Harper & Row, 1974), 523.
6 Win Arn and Donald McGavran, *Church Growth Principles* (Bayswater, Australia: Vital Publications, 1976), 87.

Chapter 28

1 'Helping people to step over the threshold', *Baptist Times*, 7 October 2004.
2 'Town centre churches are different', *Baptist Times*, 7 April 2004.

Chapter 29

1 'Evangelism is a process', *Baptist Times*, 24 February 2005.

Chapter 30

1 'Christmas is good news for all', *Baptist Times*, 23 December 2004.
2 *Christianity and Renewal*, January 2002.
3 Robert Schuller, *Your Church Has Real Possibilities* (Glendale, CA: Regal, 1974), 85.

Chapter 31

1 J. B. Phillips, *Ring of Truth: A Translator's Testimony* (London: Hodder & Stoughton, 1967), 11.
2 'A thought for Epiphany', *Baptist Times*, 6 January 2005.
3 E. V. Rieu, *The Gospels* (Harmondsworth: Penguin, 1952).
4 John B. Taylor, *Preaching through the Prophets* (Oxford: Mowbray, 1983), 13.

Chapter 32

1 'Hospitality beats friendliness', *Baptist Times*, 20 November 2003.

Chapter 33

1 'Presenting the challenge of overseas mission', *Baptist Times*, 12 August 2004.

Chapter 34

1 'How much money should we give away?', *Baptist Times*, 14 October 2004.

Chapter 35

1 'Power in the church', *Baptist Times*, 3 March 2005.
2 Quoted by William Barclay, *Gospel of Matthew*, vol. 1, 2nd ed., Daily Study Bible (Edinburgh: St Andrew Press, 1958), 91.

Chapter 36

1 'Is there a place for the church magazine?', *Baptist Times*, 26 August 2004.

2 Max Warren, *Crowded Canvas* (London: Hodder & Stoughton, 1974), quoted by Robert Patterson (ed.), *Monarch Book of Christian Wisdom* (Crowborough: Monarch, 1997), 54.

Chapter 37

1 'The demise of the midweek prayer meeting', *Baptist Times*, 2 September 2004.

Chapter 38

1 'Do we need elders as well as deacons?', *Baptist Times*, 9 September 2004.

2 John Adair, *Effective Leadership* (London: Pan, 1983), 51.

Chapter 39

1 'Team values', *Baptist Times*, 27 January 2005.

2 Howard Clinebell, *Growth Groups*, 2nd ed. (Nashville: Abingdon, 1977), 20–21.

Chapter 40

1 'Why every church member should have an appraisal', *Baptist Times*, 16 December 2004.

Chapter 41

1 'Buildings are a good investment in mission', *Baptist Times*, 17 February 2005.

Chapter 42

1 'Is there one right way to worship?', *Baptist Times*, 8 July 2004.

Chapter 43

1 'Bring back the Bible', *Baptist Times*, 29 August 2004.

2 *Apology* 1.65.

Chapter 44

1 'Let's make our churches child-friendly', *Baptist Times*, 10 June 2004.

Chapter 45

1 'How long for a sermon?', *Baptist Times*, 9 April 2004.
2 H. D. Bastian, cited by Klaas Runia, *The Sermon under Attack* (Exeter: Paternoster, 1983), 9.

Chapter 46

1 'Thank God Low Sunday can become High Sunday', *Baptist Times*, 2 December 2004.

Chapter 47

1 N. T. Wright, *The Resurrection of the Son of God* (London: SPCK, 2003), 709.
2 Pinchas Lapide, *The Resurrection of Jesus: A Jewish Perspective* (London: SPCK, 1984), 131.
3 Quoted by Michael Green, *The Day Death Died* (Leicester: IVP, 1982), 15.

Chapter 48

1 'Why we need to celebrate harvest', *Baptist Times*, 27 September 2004.

Chapter 49

1 'Preaching about money', *Baptist Times*, 21 October 2004.

Chapter 50

1 'Should we still be tithing?', *Baptist Times*, 26 February 2004.
2 Quoted by Roger Patterson, *Monarch Book of Christian Wisdom* (Crowborough: Monarch, 1997), 114.
3 Quoted by Peter Maiden, *Take my Plastic* (Carlisle: OM Publishing, 1997), 80.